INFLUENCING

INFLUENCING

Skills and Techniques for Business Success

Fiona Elsa Dent
and
Mike Brent

First published in 2006 by
PALGRAVE MACMILLAN
Houndmills, Basingstoke, Hampshire RG21 6XS and
175 Fifth Avenue, New York, N.Y. 10010
Companies and representatives throughout the world.

PALGRAVE MACMILLAN is the global academic imprint of the Palgrave
Macmillan division of St. Martin's Press, LLC and of Palgrave Macmillan Ltd.
Macmillan® is a registered trademark in the United States, United Kingdom
and other countries. Palgrave is a registered trademark in the European
Union and other countries.

ISBN-13: 978–1–4039–9668–8
ISBN-10: 1–4039–9668–7

This book is printed on paper suitable for recycling and made from fully
managed and sustained forest sources. Logging, pulping and manufacturing
processes are expected to conform to the environmental regulations of the
country of origin.

A catalogue record for this book is available from the British Library.

Library of Congress Cataloging-in-Publication Data

Dent, Fiona Elsa.
     Influencing : skills and techniques for business success / by Fiona Elsa Dent &
Mike Brent.
        p. cm.
     Includes bibliographical references and index.
     ISBN 1–4039–9668–7 (cloth)
        1. Industrial psychology. 2. Influence (Psychology) 3. Organizational
behaviour. 4. Management. I. Brent, Mike. II. Title.

HF5548.8.D454 2006
650.1—dc22   2006045711

10 9 8 7 6 5 4 3 2
15 14 13 12 11 10 09 08 07

Printed and bound in China

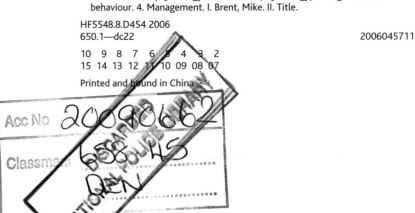

Contents

Acknowledgements

We would like to thank all our colleagues and friends at Ashridge for their support while writing this book. The following people who have all actively contributed to the content of our book deserve a special mention: Eddie Blass, Judy Curd, Karen Moyle, Angelita Orbea, Nigel Melville, Tony Cram, Richard Olivier and Richard Bamsey for the graphics, and all participants on the Influencing Skills Programmes we have run in recent years. Thanks especially to those whose interesting quotes we have used in this book.

Acknowledgements

1 Introduction

The Importance of Influencing

> *He who wishes to exert a useful influence must be careful to insult nothing. Let him not be troubled by what seems absurd but concentrate his energies to the creation of what is good. He must not demolish but build.*
>
> Goethe 1749–1832

In our work at Ashridge we meet hundreds of managers from all over the world. They all face many different issues in their work, but one common theme seems to have emerged over the past few years – whatever their position. The ability to influence and communicate effectively with both colleagues and external partners has become a crucial skill. These managers talk to us about the need to be able to influence when they have no formal authority, or what to do when they have moved from a position where they once had that authority but don't have it any more. One manager explained that she had formerly worked in an organisation and a country where she had formal authority and could tell people what to do. Now she works for a company where that formal authority simply does not work. She has to learn new ways of communication and influencing, and to be honest, it is not an easy thing to do.

Others are very open and honest about their lack of flexibility or their lack of knowledge about how to communicate effectively and influence others. One manager came on our influencing Programme at Ashridge, as he put it, 'to have the rough edges knocked off me'. Another to, 'become more rounded'.

There are different levels of influencing – the personal level and the organisational level. In this book we are more concerned with the personal level, though we will touch on some aspects of organisational influencing. The personal level applies both within and outside the company.

You can influence one to one inside the company and outside, you can influence groups of people both inside and outside the company.

Why influencing is important

There are more and more linkages between organisations both nationally and internationally. Co-operation, joint ventures, mergers and acquisitions are all increasing. As a result there is more diversity within the organisational context, and more ways of perceiving issues and events. Together with the ever increasing flow of information and increasingly faster rates of change, this means that it is virtually impossible to predict with any certainty what the right course of action is in any given situation. We could say that we live in a chaotic and complex world where success is dependent upon the development of coping strategies for the broad range of different people and situations we encounter. No one approach or style is enough, there are rarely right and wrong ways of doing things, simply different ways and this is where influencing comes in.

The fact that organisations are forced to confront increased diversity means that they have to consider many different perspectives on one issue. The ethnocentric view of the world is being increasingly challenged at the highest levels. Managers from different parts of the world want to express their perspectives, be listened to and taken seriously. This has implications for the structures of our organisations, as well as for the personal skills and competences of our managers. So, to succeed in today's turbulent working environment, professional skills together with technical competence are no longer sufficient – other less tangible skills are required. The skill of influencing and working with others is vital and should be an integral part of every manager's toolkit.

As organisations move from the industrial sector to the service sector, not only are internal relationships between employers, employees and colleagues vital, but so are relations with the clients, suppliers and other external bodies. There are more and more opportunities to interact with clients and these interactions become the focal point for the client. If the interaction is not positive, the client is lost or at best, disappointed. In the course of these interactions, communication becomes a key issue, and specifically, the obligation to influence effectively becomes of paramount importance. You cannot order your clients to do something, neither can you force your colleagues to do something against their will, and you certainly cannot oblige your boss to agree with your point of view!

Since managing is essentially achieving results through others, the most likely way of doing this is through the ability to influence people.

Most work in organisations is now carried out by groups or teams of people, and as organisations relinquish central power and hierarchical chains of command, the ability to influence – rather than command – others becomes necessary.

In working with literally thousands of managers on various influencing programmes, workshops and sessions there are a range of recurring themes which emerge as the motivators for them to seek to explore and develop their approach to influencing. These themes fall into three broad categories:

▶ **Dealing with transitions**
▶ **Managing complexity**
▶ **Influencing agility**

THE IMPORTANCE OF INFLUENCING AND BEING OPEN TO INFLUENCE

THE CHALLENGER CASE

In late 1985 and early 1986 The North American Space Agency (NASA) was preparing the launch of their eleventh manned mission – Challenger – with a crew of seven, including two woman, into space. The crew were – Francis Scobee, Michael Smith, Ellison Onizuka, Judith Resnik, Ronald McNair, Christa McAuliffe and Gregory Jarvis. Christa McAuliffe was a teacher and about to be the first civilian into space.

The launch date was delayed due to bad weather and NASA was under pressure to launch quickly. However an engineer called Roger Boisjoly and some of his colleagues at supplier Thiokol feared that a small component – called an O ring – on the shuttle would not stand up to the cold tempera-ture. They argued that it was best to delay launch till the weather was warmer. They feared the worst – a disastrous failure leading to loss of life. In Boisjoly's own words, 'It was away from goodness' to launch when there was such a major risk. In a tele -conference with NASA, Thiokol management first of all recommended to NASA that the shuttle not be launched below 53 degrees. NASA did not receive this well and they asked George Hardy (Marshalls Space Center's deputy director of Science and Engineering)for his decision. He said he was 'appalled' at Thiokol's decision but would not authorise a launch over a contractor's objection.

Then followed an offline discussion among Thiokol's people where Thiokol's General Manager told his Vice President of Engineering that he needed to, 'take off his engineering hat and put on his management hat'. The four senior executives at Thiokol then made a decision to support the launch, completely excluding from this decision the engineers who had argued for a delay.

The engineer Roger Boisjoly says that at that moment, 'I felt totally helpless and felt that further argument was fruitless, so I too stopped pressing my case', He was so upset with the decision that he doesn't remember one of the NASA team asking if anyone had anything else to say. NASA then accepted Thiokol senior managers decision not to delay the launch.

It was unfortunate for the crew of Apollo and their families, that NASA did not heed the supplier's engineers' warnings. NASA was under pressure to launch the shuttle, disregarded the warnings and launched with catastrophic consequences – the loss of the spacecraft and all those on board. The Presidential Commission into the accident concluded that 'the decision to launch was flawed', that 'the decision making process was flawed in several ways' and that the 'testimony of those involved reveals a failure in communication' (Chapter 5 of Report)

So where was the responsibility? With NASA who disregarded the engineers advice ? With the project manager at Marshall, who put forth the case for launch 'with a very strong and forthright rationale'? With senior management at Morton Thiokol? (they were concerned that they would lose NASA business. The Presidential Commission concluded that Thiokol management reversed its position and recommended launch at the urging of Marshall Space Center and contrary to the views of its engineers in order to accommodate a major customer).

Or could it be said that Thiokols's engineers did not set their case out convincingly enough? Clearly from an ethical perspective the engineers behaved impeccably and the Presidential Commission reported that the launch decision was flawed, but if we look at how influential they were in such an important issue, could they have been more effective in influencing their senior management at Thiokol and the NASA project managers?

This case is often presented as an ethical case study but in our opinion it clearly illustrates the importance both of influencing, and being open to being influenced by others.

We could ask if the engineers were influential enough, and also if the Thiokol senior management and NASA were open enough to being influenced. Or were they too quick to close down arguments because of the pressure they felt? Thiokol to keep their client happy, and NASA because of the pressure they felt to launch the Challenger.

As stated above, one of the Thiokol managers asked a senior engineer to 'take off your engineer's hat and put on your management hat!'

He is in effect influencing the senior engineer to disregard his concerns about safety and to focus on issues like profit. The NASA managers in their teleconference with Thiokol used language like, 'The Shuttle has flown 19 times and come back 19 times!' and 'My God, Thiokol, when do you want me to launch? In April?' Their language puts pressure on the supplier's management and engineers to accept launching, even though the supplier's management team has been told about their engineers concern. Boisjoly tells us that he was screaming at his managers during their internal meeting. Boisjoly has been concerned about this issue for many months. He has tried to influence his own management team, but in his own words they have not taken him seriously enough. (he says 'it was like talking to a solid piece of granite') It is interesting to watch the videos and documentaries made of this and read the Presidential Commission report. It seems to us that the influencing style was very much a data driven one.

The engineers were convinced that the O ring would not operate safely at low temperatures but of course they were unable to 'prove' this. So they tried to show charts and data to convince NASA but NASA wanted proof. Clearly the engineers cannot possibly *prove* this, so they were unable to effectively influence NASA. In fact they should not even have had to prove it – just demonstrate that the shuttle was not safe. Normally the onus is on the contractor to prove that it is safe. Thiokol were not able to *prove* this to NASA and this illustrates NASA's unwillingness to be influenced in this matter. Roger Boisjoly told a Channel 4 documentary that although he had warned his own management about the problem, and they finally agreed to set up a task force to look at the problem, he was given 'no power, no authority, no resources and no management support.'

What might the engineers have done to convince NASA? Obviously they could not prove that the Challenger spacecraft would fail, so they needed to convince NASA of the dangers and consequences.

It is far easier to look back with hindsight, but it seems clear to us that the engineers could have tried different approaches. They did not appear to use any visioning, they did not paint a picture of what would happen if the component failed. They did not make use of the fact that millions of schoolchildren were watching the launch live on TV to see school teacher McAulife be the first teacher in space. When NASA manager Larry Mulloy asked Thiokol if they wanted him to launch in April the engineers might have said, 'Yes if that's what it takes to bring our seven astronauts home safely!'

(*Sources*: Case Western Online Ethics Center for Engineering and Science; Report of the Presidential Commission on the Space Shuttle Challenger Accident June 1986; Channel 4 Documentary, 2/2/06)

In addition to the three themes almost all managers mention their awareness of the importance of the soft skills and in particular the need to be more emotionally intelligent.

The engineers did not ask NASA to reflect on how badly their public relation exercise in getting a teacher into space would backfire if the challenger failed because of a defective component which they already knew about. They did not point out that if the mission failed and there was loss of life that this wouldn't just delay the mission till April but for years.

They did not point out the effect on the American public of the deaths of these seven heroes, including two women, one of whom was a schoolteacher with the eyes of the nation upon her!

What is intensely interesting is that, despite the massive potential loss and damage, one of Thiokol's engineers said (Presidential Commission 1986) that he truly believed that there was no point in him doing anything further than what he had already attempted to do, because he believed in management's right to take the input of an engineer and then make a decision. Even though he feared loss of life he was still prepared to allow management to override him.

All in all the engineers at Thiokol did everything in their power to stop the launch. We might in retrospect point out that they could have used different influencing techniques, and been more effective influencers, but the main issue is the unwillingness of their managers and of NASA managers to listen and be open to being influenced by the engineers. They obviously did not want the accident to happen, but their desire to push for the launch was greater than their concerns. They in effect changed the rules by asking the suppliers' engineers to prove that the shuttle was dangerous instead of asking them to prove that it was safe to fly.

This demonstrates to us the necessity of being able to convince and communicate effectively when you do not have formal authority. And the corollary – of being open to being influenced when you do have formal power and authority.

Dealing with transitions

The transitions that people mention include:

▶ **Moving from line management to general management** As a line manager one tends to have good knowledge of the people and the processes in your sphere of influence. However many people find the move to general management rather daunting when not only will you get involved with discussions about topics on which you are not an authority but also you may be influencing people over whom you have no authority.

▶ **Changing from a functional role to a corporate role** As a functional specialist you may well be the authority on the area of your expertise; the move to a corporate role rather like the move into general management means involvement with topics about which you may have little knowledge or understanding and you will also undoubtedly be influencing people over whom you have no authority.

▶ **Going from a mono culture to multi culture** The move from a national culture to an international culture is one way of looking at this or it could be that you work in an organisation that has been merged, taken over or entered into various joint ventures – for whatever reason, the scenario you now work in a broader cultural situation. Recognising, managing and influencing in any of these environments is challenging

▶ **Coping with the change of working within one team to multiple teams** The move from leading or working within one team to being in charge of or working as part of several teams adds a level of complexity to many people's lives. In business life today it is becoming more and more common to be a part of several teams and therefore to have to deal with multiple relationships, all at different levels. Typically teams today are made up of people whose skills fit with the needs of the team and therefore you can find yourself in teams where people come from all sorts of different professions and levels within the organisation.

▶ **Dealing with the differences between hierarchical and matrix organisations** Many of us are increasingly working in less structured environments where we are expected to work in several different work groups often across functions. In this type of situation levels of authority and responsibility are often not made explicit and therefore the ability to influence becomes a key skill.

Managing complexity

We read and hear a lot about the ever increasingly complex environment in which we all operate today, and our participants tell us there are many aspects of this complexity that affect their ability to influence. These include:

▶ **The complexity of relationships** – It is not just the personality differences but the multitude of other differences, for instance, cultural, multi-generational, differing motivators, needs and wants, etc …

▶ **Influencing without authority** – This is a much recurring theme from many who attend our sessions. The challenge for so many of us is to exert influence upon those over whom we have no line authority. This of course is one of the key challenges for the successful influencer – to gain commitment without using authority and power.

▶ **Managing upwards** – It is a challenge for many people and not just managing their own boss but also managing people at more senior levels in the organisation or other authority figures in life.

▶ **Across boundaries** – national, international, functional, professional etc … Again the complexity of dealing with multiple stakeholders from many different backgrounds and with very different expectations and experience.

▶ **Virtually** – This occurs when influencing is not face to face. So many influencing discussions now take place over the internet, telephone and in tele-conferences. In virtual environments you lose an element of the communication process and therefore have to be even more aware of how you are being perceived by others using the remaining processes.

▶ **Multiple different stakeholders** – So many of us now recognise that influencing is not a one shot effort with one person but a process which will frequently involve multiple different stakeholders many of whom are not always obvious at the start.

Influencing agility

Another huge challenge for so many of us is the need to be particularly agile in influencing others, or put another way 'influencing in the moment'. The technological age in which we live demands much quicker response rates and immediacy. Our skill and approach to influencing have clearly been affected by this.

▶ **Immediacy** – the ability to focus on the people and issue at hand. Challenging our skill in switching from one event to another and giving it our full attention.

▶ **Speed of response and reaction** – people are used to getting immediate results and so often expect this in all sorts of situations.

▶ **Getting it right** – many of us worry about our capability to 'get things right'. There is so often an expectation that we will get things right first time because there simply isn't time to get things wrong!

▶ **Choosing the right style and approach** – again there isn't time to get it wrong so, we must be both aware and agile enough to select the correct style and approach for each person and situation.

What this has all led to is a heightened awareness of the need for the softer social skills and emotional intelligence when influencing. We hope that while this book may not solve all these issues it will help you to deal with them and give you a range of ideas to try out and to develop and improve your skills.

But, before we go any further …

What do we mean by influence?

The word comes from the Latin 'Influere' meaning 'to flow in'. The original meaning of the word influence was as an ethereal fluid thought to flow out from the stars and to affect the actions of man – as in the moon influencing the tides.

We would define influence as the ability to affect others attitudes, beliefs and behaviours without using force or formal authority. Many of our participants have asked us whether we think influencing others is somehow bad, to which we reply that influencing is a natural process – we all influence all the time, whether it is consciously or unconsciously. We are programmed to influence others and there is nothing intrinsically bad about influencing as long as it is not used to manipulate others nor has a deleterious effect on others.

Think of a baby – when a baby is hungry she cries in order to attract our attention to the fact that she is hungry. We notice and then feed or change her or make sure she is comfortable. Is this communication influence or manipulation? For us this is a simple genetic programming of survival. We as parents are programmed to respond to the crying.

Think of what would happen if you never influenced anyone! In fact can you even think of anyone who has not influenced someone in some way in their life? It's simply not possible!

One of the questions we pose to our participants on our Influencing Skills Programmes is 'What do you think makes a good influencer?' Here are some of the responses:

▶ 'Someone that puts their point of view in such a way that others feel inclined to buy into it.'
▶ 'Someone who can open minds and enable people to think new ideas.'
▶ 'A person who makes things happen for the right reasons'.
▶ 'An individual that can tailor their approach to influence others with ease and do so seamlessly'.
▶ 'A good influencer is someone who is able to get results by understanding how decisions are made, gaining buy-in from the appropriate people and mobilising a team to achieve the desired outcome.'
▶ 'Someone who can make the point without stabbing anyone with it'.
▶ 'One who is able to persuade others round to their way of thinking using a variety of techniques to suit the situation'.
▶ 'A person who is self assured, knows what he wants and how to achieve it, has a credible reputation, is sensitive to others' emotions and views, shows enthusiasm, conviction and inspiration'.

Influence v. manipulation

Debate often arises about the difference between influencing and manipulation. It is our belief that there are three key differences:

▶ The aim or the goal – if the aim is simply to get your own way irrespective of the others' opinion then we are talking about manipulation.
▶ If the goal is to have a negative outcome for the other person then it is also manipulation. This is often also referred to as a win/lose outcome.
▶ If you lie during the process then this is also manipulation.

Manipulation is therefore an exploitative process where an individual is actively taking advantage of a situation for their own benefit.

"Instead of using authority or manipulation to get someone to do something, influencing helps people to realise that there is genuine advantage to them in moving in the direction you want. Influencing creates buy-in and less resistance long-term. It engenders creativity and co-operation and rather than obedience potential resistance."

Nicola Thomas, a former Marketing
Director of Christian Salvesen

We feel that it is quite arrogant for people to say that we do not need to influence others. To live is to influence! We have heard managers say that they are often right but that their people don't listen to them! So what do you do? Change your people or change yourself – or at least your approach? Another way of looking at this argument is this – if you are not going to influence at work, what ARE you going to do? Researchers into communication point out that almost all exchanges between people involve some element of Influence (Hargie and Dickson 2004).

Influencing and persuading

We are often asked if there is a difference between Influencing and persuading. The terms are often used interchangeably, but there are some key differences; Sanders and Fitch (2001) argues that persuasion is influence when there is resistance, while influence is achieved by offering inducements that make it expedient for someone to do something.

Another distinction according to Hargie and Dickson (2004) is that persuasion always involves influencing but influence does not always involve persuasion. In other words you can influence by means other than persuasion.

One final distinction is about success. Persuasion implies success, whereas influence may just be an attempt. You cannot say 'I persuaded them but they did not do it!', whereas it is possible to say, 'I influenced them but they didn't do it'. Here influence may mean that they listened to me, or modified their position or perspective somewhat, but did not actually make any behavioural changes. However it may represent a shift in attitude which could lead to behavioural change further down the line.

People will not do what you want if they don't know what you want – so there is a clear basis for at least communicating what you want. You can do this in two ways. One is to tell or order people to do what you want. This may work for some people in some companies some of the time, but generally it's not an effective way of getting things done any more. And even if you do use this approach there are skilled and unskilled ways of doing it (more on this later).

So how do you get things done if you don't tell people? You need to get their commitment to doing something they perhaps were not originally going to do – in other words you are going to try to influence them to see things from your perspective!

A further argument in favour of using an influencing style rather than a command or tell-one is that it builds sustainable leadership. When you order someone to do something, you are building in the necessity to keep on giving orders, and if you rely too much on formal power you run the risk of getting employee compliance rather than employee commitment.

Power is not just about owning or possessing things. We believe power is actually more about relationships than it is about things. Ultimately, execution and completion of tasks is dependent on subordinate action. This suggests that power relationships are essentially relationships of negotiation, or as we would put it – relationships of influence. Put simply, influence is a form of power, but one which depends on personal characteristics more than formal authority.

Use of formal power therefore is neither effective nor efficient, control leads in the end to dependency, but by influencing you devolve power to the influencee. This of course implies that the influencer must be open to being influenced. If you only ever want to be the influencer, then you are commanding and telling, but under a different name!

In effect, a large part of a manager's job is to discuss things with peers and bosses, and, is not just about the simple delivery of orders to subordinates. In this type of situation, negotiating or influencing skills become paramount, because the option of using formal power is no longer available. As Levesque (1995) said 'Leadership involves influencing the way others think in order to influence their behaviour'.

The main focus of this book is to help you review and reflect upon how you perform as an influencer to discuss and review skills, styles, approaches and techniques. We have developed a model which should help to make sense of the whole process and it is around this model that we have built this book.

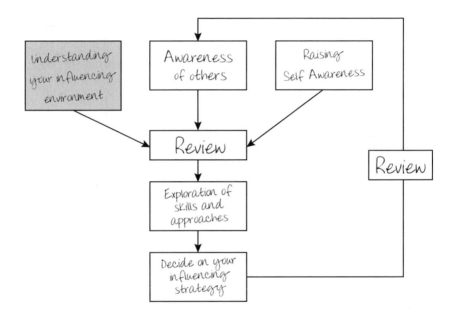

A MODEL FOR INFLUENCING

We believe strongly that influencing is a process not an event. This means that you have to be aware of the impact you are having on others when involved in any interaction with them as it will always affect their perception of you and thus their willingness to be influenced by you. Each of the sections of the model will be covered in a chapter of the book.

In the next chapter we start by exploring and developing what we mean by the influencing environment. Understanding and awareness of your influencing environment is vital to your success. Whatever the environment, from a large organisation to a small family unit, understanding and being aware of what behaviour and approaches are acceptable and unacceptable is essential. In business this is sometimes known as the 'culture' of the organisation where culture is defined as 'the way we do things around here'.

We then move on to explore self awareness. First of all we examine issues to do with influencing skill by establishing the key competences and describing the behaviours and capabilities which contribute to these competences. In particular we focus on those skills which contribute to the emotional element of influencing and we encourage you to review and reflect on your strengths, weaknesses and development needs. In the next chapter we look at influencing style. Typically we all have a preference in terms of our influencing style and this is the approach we tend to rely on in the majority of situations. However, over reliance on one style can mean that you are putting yourself at a disadvantage in certain situations with certain people. We will introduce you to our model of influencing style and explore the key characteristics and uses of each of the different styles.

Understanding other people and reading them correctly is vital for an effective outcome in most influencing situations. So the next stage in this process requires you to look at the other people involved. This means gathering as much information as possible about *all* the other people who are either involved or affected by your influencing issue. By adopting some simple planning and preparatory techniques and becoming more aware of others needs, wants and style we have a fuller picture of our influencing challenge.

At this stage you should have sufficient data to begin a first review process to analyse and review your environment, yourself and your influencee's and to begin to formulate your thoughts for the way ahead.

You should now be in a position to think about the influencing approaches and techniques to use. This may involve a variety of different approaches for different people in different situations all of whom are being affected by your issue. In this section we will explore and examine a variety of different tools and techniques which may be useful.

The final phase of the model is to decide upon the most appropriate strategy to adopt for the situation, people and issue. We will examine a range of different approaches that you may adopt when beginning to implement your influencing strategy.

Finally we will bring things to a close by highlighting the three key messages for success, eight common misconceptions and the ten top tips which we believe contribute to influencing success in today's business and social context.

One word of warning – this book does not just set out tools and techniques for influencing. It takes the position that Influence is a two way process and that in order to be effective, managers must be prepared to be influenced as well as to influence. If you are not open to being influenced and flexible in your needs and approach you are unlikely to be a strong and effective influencer. Influencing is as much about attitude, values and relationships as it is about tools techniques and strategies. Companies talk more and more about empowerment but rarely put it into practise. If we really are to empower people in organisations, it means that managers will have to give up some of their own power, and be open to being influenced by their peers, subordinates and clients, as well as learning to be skilful influencers themselves.

2 Understanding Your Influencing Environment

The Big Picture

> *Moving from the public sector to private sector has made me realise that influencing is as much about the situation as the people!*
>
> Ashridge participant on Influencing Strategies and Skills Programme

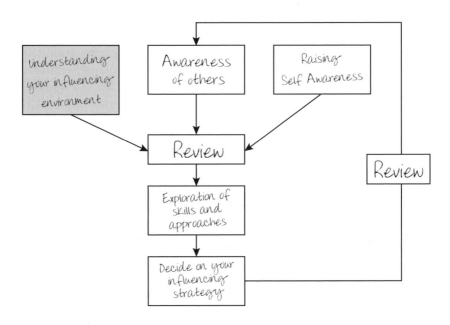

A MODEL FOR INFLUENCING

Understanding and awareness of your influencing environment is vital to your success. What works in one business context may or may not work in another. Like all aspects of influencing this takes thought, analysis and awareness. Another way of looking at this is to recognise that influencing is situational or contextual; if you are trying to influence someone (about the same topic) the environmental context will have an effect on how you go about it. So for instance, let's say you are attempting to influence colleagues about a new expenses policy. The way you would go about this in a small family business will be very different to the approach you might take in a large multi national; similarly how you may influence your HR colleagues will vary from how you may influence the Sales Managers. It's all about the context.

In examining the context one also has to consider the span of the issue. For instance, is the issue on which you are attempting to influence personal, internal and local? Or, might it have wider ramifications in which case you may need to consider the implications for the whole department, division, organisation or in extreme cases your particular business sector. As we said earlier it's all contextual and therefore appropriate that one always reflects upon the extent of the issue in addition to the people involved. Time spent in reflection, preparation and planning is vital to the success of any influencing discussion – whether it is a simple issue or a highly complex one involving multiple stakeholders.

In examining one's environment there are a variety of situational contexts to consider:

▶ The current business/social environment
▶ The various cultural issues
  ▷ National
  ▷ Organisational
  ▷ Divisional/departmental
  ▷ Professional

It's all about consciousness of what might work and what won't work in your particular context and situation.

The current business and social environment

Today's business world is a complex, ever changing and often chaotic environment. In addition to this for many of us our organisations work in a global context all of which makes our influencing arena very challenging.

Depending upon the influencing issue, some of the things you should consider in relation to the wider business and social contexts are:

▶ The prevailing economic climate – are things booming or is there a recession? Either of these will almost certainly have an effect on your approach and process. So for instance, your organisation is currently operating in a period of cost constraint due to a sluggish market. However, you want to give your team an end of year bonus as they have been working extremely hard all year to win loads of business. To be able to do this you have to influence and gain the support of your colleagues and boss. In view of the economic situation it may not be the best time to approach this issue and you may have to reward the team in some other way.

▶ How competitive is your business situation, whether your organisation is operating in a highly competitive market or in a more monopolistic situation.

▶ If you are operating in a global business, reflect about the type of people you employ – their nationalities, their experience, their training, their age, their gender, their professions and are they working locally or are they working in an expatriate situation. An example of this is when a friend of ours took on an overseas assignment to work in Florida. Now many of us might be forgiven for thinking this shouldn't be too challenging from a multi cultural perspective, thinking it probably involved mainly US citizens and a few expatriate British people. The reality was actually very different. The actual team in the office was predominantly of Hispanic origin from many different cultures including Mexicans, Cubans, Caribbeans and few Native Americans and Britons. So, a truly international office. The challenges were multiple, not the least among them being language. Often the major business language was Spanish not English as one would expect. What our friend experienced and learned was he had to take account of each individual and their particular set of cultural needs in addition to their personal needs.

▶ Review the societal values and processes operating currently and reflect upon how these might affect your approach. So for instance, many people in the UK today have a different attitude to work – very hard working and wanting a greater sense of work life balance throughout their careers – taking longer holidays, regular sabbaticals and even career breaks. Again such changes have to be taken into account when influencing.

Additionally some typical world issues which may have an impact on how you will influence include:

▶ The Iraq war
▶ Changes in leadership in any of the major governments or states
▶ Natural disasters – the tsunami in the Far East, the hurricane and flooding in New Orleans, etc…
▶ Terrorist attacks – 9/11, the bombings in London and Madrid.

► Changes at the top of your organisation
► Stock market crashes

Obviously these issues will be contextual and will only be of importance when you are on a strategic level for instance: take both the tsunami which occurred in the Far East in 2004 and the hurricane in New Orleans in 2005 and imagine that you work in the travel industry. Both these events could have an impact on how your organisation influences people to buy holidays in these areas in the foreseeable future.

The important issue is not to forget about this bigger picture or the world we operate in and how this might have an effect upon your approach and/or issue.

Exercise

You might like to think about your own business context and reflect upon the external business and societal issues that might have an effect upon your influencing approach. For instance:

► How might world conditions affect your staff travelling internationally?
► Thinking about your industry what political/climatic/security events might be having an effect upon how you do business?
► How might individuals with differing moral values and beliefs have an impact?

The various cultural issues

Cultural differences have a significant effect on how we do business and therefore will play an important part in how we approach any influencing situation. The effect of cultural differences on how we manage and lead in our business world is a topic in its own right and is well written about by several authors, for instance, Charles Handy (1985) and Fons Trompenaars and Charles Hampden-Turner (1997).

In relation to influencing there is however some basic elements of culture that we need to consider on a day to day basis. These aspects of culture can help us to plan and prepare effectively for the various situations we find ourselves in. In our experience the most important aspects of culture are those relating to national cultures, organisational cultures and professional cultures. Before we examine each of these areas let's first define what we mean by culture. At its simplest we can define culture as 'the way we do things around here', with here being this country, this organisation, this department in this job or profession. It's all about the beliefs, norms, values and the typical patterns of behaviour that are adhered to by the particular group being described.

So, for instance if we were to look at national culture we would probably find that if a group of Chinese people were getting together for a night out their behaviour may be very different and demonstrate very different behavioural norms to those of a typical group of Britons.

Let us illustrate with a small example. We recently attended a 'typical' Chinese banquet in the UK where the audience was a mix of Chinese and British business people. Apart from the obvious differences relating to the food and eating implements, chop sticks rather than forks and knives, and lots of different choices of food, beer with the meal rather than wine, many different dishes to select from at the table rather than starter, main course and pudding, there were a couple of other rather obvious differences that struck us. The first of these was in relation to what we saw as formality in the situation and the number of short speeches that took place at the beginning, and towards the end of the evening. The second was the custom of toasting each other. During the whole meal small groups of Chinese people would move round the room toasting one another's health, with much glass clinking, emptying of the glass you were drinking from and bowing. The third difference that struck us was that when the banquet was over, following a final thank you speech, everyone got up and immediately left the room and the venue.

These are small differences which made for an interesting learning experience and social evening and in such a social setting probably had little affect upon our ability to influence this group. However, imagine if this had been the beginning of a joint venture meeting and the banquet was the kick off event and the next day business meetings were to start where the various managers had to work together to influence one another about the way ahead for the joint venture. Then, what we learned and how we behaved during that meeting might have a significant effect upon the process the next day.

This example illustrates some of the cultural differences between countries. But, what we must also consider are the differences between organisations, professions and departments. In our role as Ashridge Faculty members we do a lot of selling to potential clients from many different organisations in both the public and private sectors and both nationally and internationally. What we have found is that understanding and considering an organisation's culture can help us enormously in preparing our 'pitch'. So for instance, typically in the public sector the written proposal will be very formal and structured and will often be in relation to a formal tender process, while in the private sector many clients are happy with a short Powerpoint slide presentation as their written proposal. It's all about doing your homework and getting it right for the needs of the client. In this type of case the rules and processes the organisation has established over many years (the organisation's culture) are dictating the approaches they will find acceptable.

So, in terms of cultural differences here are some of the key areas to consider when preparing to influence others about your issue.

NATIONAL CULTURAL DIFFERENCES

The whole area of national cultures is an interesting and well researched area in itself and you can explore this in greater detail in many books and papers. If you want to look in real depth at this issue you might find the books 'Culture's Consequences' by G. Hofstede, 'Riding The Waves of Culture' by Fons Trompenaars and Charles Hampden-Turner useful; alternatively if you simply want a general overview of the issue Management Pocketbook's 'The Cross Cultural Business Pocketbook' by John Mattock and the 'Cultural Gaffes Pocketbook' by Angelena Boden are both useful.

Understanding national cultures is exceedingly difficult. So, for instance, even though there are certain norms or accepted ways of behaving when dealing with different nationalities these will also be affected by the particular individual's or group of individual's own personality, experience and current situation. So, while you may be able to say all Scots (we are both Scottish, so we feel qualified to get away with this!) are 'careful with their money' this is simply a generalisation used to describe a nation that simply is not true. There are many such generalisations relating to different national cultures – these you must consider with care. As with all cultural differences each individual has their own DNA which will affect their overall behaviour and reactions to different situations.

The key issue is to recognise some of the challenges you might experience when influencing in an international and cross cultural situation. If you do find yourself influencing in a multinational setting some of the things you should consider include:

▶ The language or languages all the participants speak and their level of fluency in the language you will be using while doing business
▶ Their role in the organisation and their level in the hierarchy
▶ Their level of familiarity with you
▶ How they might perceive you – more senior/junior, expert/generalist, decision maker/influencer, etc...
▶ The approach to decision making in their day to day business context
▶ Your past experience of the individuals or their colleagues

Language alone can be a significant barrier – even when we are all speaking the same language there is plenty of room for misunderstanding!

ORGANISATIONAL CULTURAL DIFFERENCES

Organisational or corporate culture will certainly affect the approach you use when influencing. Very often different organisational cultures will support different influencing styles – that isn't to say a breadth of styles exists within the organisation, however, you may find that certain styles prevail and are more successful.

There are two models of corporate cultural difference that we find useful when discussing this with our clients and participants. The first one was developed by the psychologist Roger Harrison and he describes four cultural types and the second one, developed by Charles Handy and based on Harrison's original work, uses the analogies of Greek Gods to describe the various cultures:

▶ **The Power Culture** is often found in small entrepreneurial organisations or areas of organisations where the culture depends upon a central source of power and can reside in an individual. Size becomes an issue for this culture as the power and creation of the cultural norms emanate from the one central source. So, high levels of trust and empathy are required between individuals and in particular these cultures put a lot of faith in powerful individuals who have track records of success and others are aware of this and therefore will follow willingly. People in this organisation are likely to be loyal to individuals and therefore to be influenced by their vision, enthusiasm and belief. Handy suggests that the God in this culture would be Zeus, the head of all the Gods in Ancient Greece and he represents this culture in a web type model. An example of a typical power culture might be the old mafia families in the US. These families were usually headed by a 'Don' who was very much the central power source making all the decisions and being very much in charge – one tended to cross such a man at one's peril. The movie series '*The Godfather*' very much illustrated this type of power culture.

▶ **The Role Culture** is often typified by bureaucratic processes where things are heavily procedural and rule bound. Role culture organisations will often have strong well espoused values, agreed processes for getting things done, consistency in approach and in general things will be pretty predictable. People in role culture organisations are likely to be influenced by rationality and logic where putting a convincing case forward will be vital. Handy's God for this culture is Apollo the god of reason and he represents this culture with a model of a Greek temple with a strong roof supported by pillars which represent the various departments. An example of a role culture might be a department in the UK civil service.

▶ **The Team Culture** exists where the organisation emphasises teams, projects and achievement. Features of this type of culture are very adaptable with teams forming and disbanding depending upon business needs at the time. People in these organisations are more likely to be influenced by experts who have a track record of success and who are task oriented and motivated by getting the job done. Handy's god in this case is Athena the warrior goddess and she represents this culture with a net indicating the importance of the matrix as its structure. An example of a typical team culture organisation is perhaps a management consultancy practice.

▶ **The Person Culture** is observed where the organisation emphasises the relationship between individuals and where a high level of harmony and support for each other exists. This is an unusual culture and can only exist where the individuals band together for the common good. Influencing in this type of culture will almost wholly depend upon participation and joint involvement where experts are recognised and taken heed of in relation to their particular area of expertise. The relevant god here is Dionysus, the god of the self orientated individual, the free spirit and is represented diagrammatically by a cluster similar to a cluster of stars. An example of a person culture might be a counselling practice, or indeed any group of professionals who band together for the common good.

These descriptions are useful to help you reflect upon the type of organisational culture that you operate in or indeed that you are attempting to influence within. However, while there may be one predominant culture it isn't always that clean cut and you may find that in different parts of the organisation different cultures prevail.

In preparing and planning how to influence in relation to your particular issue, giving consideration to these environmental and cultural issues can help you to develop your influencing process and to plan the most appropriate approach for the people involved.

Typically different cultures will have their own preferred ways of

▶ making decisions,
▶ managing and leading people,
▶ resolving conflict,
▶ planning tasks and responsibilities and
▶ influencing change

In terms of diagnosing culture you can pay attention to some or all of the following:

▶ The buildings – their age, their location, their structure, how the offices are allocated, single cabins or open plan offices, the reception area is welcoming or austere

► Annual reports – what do they talk about, achievements, people, data and financials
► How people behave – is it formal or informal; how do people greet each other – first names or not?
► How is promotion and career development dealt with – based on years of service or achievement?
► At meetings – what do people talk about is it mainly task oriented or people oriented?

All of these will give you clues about the culture and will help you to think about your approach when influencing. As always there are no right and wrong answers or approaches, it's usually all down to reflection, planning, preparation and a little bit of luck.

One example where Fiona gained significant cues and clues regarding the culture of an organisation which subsequently helped in her dealings with the client was the early meetings with a big client in the financial services sector. On the first visit to the client's offices she noticed several distinguishing features which told her a lot about the way of working in this organisation. In particular she noticed the very casual way that all employees dressed, the modern open plan offices where everyone sat, including all the senior managers, the quality of the office furniture and how it was the same for all employees, the free beverages and food at food stations, the friendly way that people greeted each other and the initial greeting at the reception area where she was given a cup of coffee as a matter of course while waiting to meet her contact. These clues indicated a role type of culture where achievement and commitment were important. It also helped her to plan the pitch for the business adopting a more informal approach which she felt would appeal to the clients more than a formal presentation. The business was won and these early clues together with additional data collected through other visits and meetings helped tremendously to build and develop a successful and long term relationship.

Exercise

You might like to reflect about your current organisation:

► How would you describe your organisation?
► What do you notice about the way things are done in the organisation?
► Overall what type of culture is it?
► What about your particular part of the organisation, is it the same as the organisation culture or are there some differences?

▶ Having analysed your responses what does this tell you about the best approaches for influencing?

You might also like to reflect about the type of culture you feel most comfortable working in and how this will affect your confidence when influencing others.

PROFESSIONAL/JOB ROLE CULTURES

Another aspect of cultural difference are those strong allegiances and patterns of behaviour that exist within professions and job roles. Many people are attracted to certain job roles or professions perhaps due to particular key responsibilities, features and aspects of the job or profession. Some professions and jobs have strong and apparent cultural features; for instance,

▶ Nursing – caring, people oriented, uniform, structured
▶ Accountancy – numerate, rational, logical, task oriented
▶ Customer Care – communication, helping, social, responsive to others' needs
▶ Police Force – rules, control, helping others, uniform
▶ TV Presenter – confident, communicative, extrovert

Obviously the people who work in these various professions and jobs will have their own preferences when being influenced. However, as influencers we need to consider not only this but the cultural features of the profession or job role as they almost certainly will have some bearing upon the way you should influence an individual.

So, you might like to consider the following in relation to the person's profession or job role:

▶ What is the purpose of the job?
▶ What are the key features of the job?
▶ What sort of people are attracted to this role?

Cultural differences are an important aspect of understanding your influencing environment and should always be considered in the preparatory stages for influencing others.

✍ **SUMMARY OF KEY POINTS**

In understanding your influencing environment there are two main aspects to consider – the current business and social environment and the different cultural issues.

Your influencee's business and social environment will almost certainly have an effect upon how they will be feeling at any given time. Time spent reflecting about the significant events which may be having an effect on your influencee prior to entering any influencing discussion will be time well spent. This will then allow you to plan how you might best take account of them when actually influencing them.

The various aspects of cultural difference are also extremely worthy of consideration; in some cases it may be that you must consider the following aspects of culture:

☛ National
☛ Organisational
☛ Professional

In others it may be that you only have to consider one aspect of culture. So, for instance you may be influencing a cross cultural team of engineers – all from the same organisation but of different nationalities – and your main concern here would be the national cultural differences.

Time spent analysing and reflecting in this area will undoubtedly contribute to more successful outcomes in the long run.

3 Influencing Skills and Attitudes

What Do You Bring to the Party?

> *The aim of argument or of discussion should not be victory, but progress*
>
> Joseph Joubert (1754–1824)
> French writer

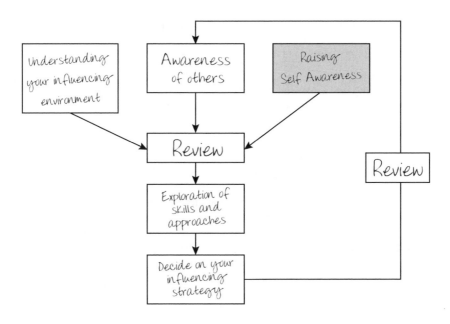

A MODEL FOR INFLUENCING

Certain key skills and attitudes are essential for effective influencing. An understanding of these skills and attitudes, together with an awareness of your own ability in the areas, is helpful for successful influencing in today's complex organisational environment.

In our work at Ashridge we have identified a range of important skills, competences and attitudes that play a significant part in successful influencing and persuading. These skills have been identified through observation of others, desk research and experience of working with thousands of managers in an influencing context. We believe there are eleven core skills that will benefit all influencers. We have incorporated these core skills into a 360° questionnaire – The Ashridge Inventory of Management Skills (AIMS) – The Emotional Element – this enables individuals to assess their own skill level and to get feedback from a range of others about their perception of the individual's skill level.

Part of the research we did was to survey participants of the Ashridge Influencing Strategies and Skills Programme and to ask them a range of questions in relation to their influencing experience. The research survey results indicate the following:

We have surveyed hundreds of participants on our Influencing Strategies and Skills Programme and in response to the question 'Please list the skills you believe to be vital for effective influencing?' the top ten answers are:

1. Communication skills,
2. Listening,
3. Reading and understanding others,
4. Flexibility/Adaptability,
5. Empathy,
6. Confidence,
7. Knowledgeable about topic,
8. Ability to make the case/articulate good arguments,
9. Persuasion and
10. Paying attention to the thoughts/objections of those being influenced.

In total 44 different skills have been expressed, all of which have been mentioned by more than one person.

The skills identified have helped us in developing the 360° Questionnaire – AIMS – The Emotional Element – which follows.

Exercise – self perception questionnaire

Before reading on you may like to assess your perception of your own skill level in each of the areas. Do this by assessing your current performance level in each area against the five measures below:

1. A skill needing considerable improvement
2. Some skills displayed but need improvement
3. Average or fair skills displayed, but not a strength
4. Above average skills displayed regularly
5. Consistent high performance in this area

Now look at the table below (which is a subset of the questionnaire AIMS – The Emotional Element) and allocate yourself a score in each of the 11 areas.

Skills description	Current performance level				
	I	2	3	4	5
Communication skills – conveys ideas and information clearly and in a manner appropriate to the audience					
Awareness of others' needs – awareness of other people, their reactions, needs, motivators and style					
Adaptability – having the flexibility to adjust your approach, language and views to suit differing influencing situations					
Networking – manages relationships in order to effectively build networks					
Conflict – deals effectively with interpersonal tensions					
Impact – shows energy and commitment to making things happen, projects confidence and 'can do' attitude, explores new options for the business and challenges the current way of operating					
Personal approach – has the desired attitudes for effective influencing – trust, credibility, risk taker, enthusiasm and patience					
Persuasiveness – persuades and influences in a way that gains commitment, tailoring approach when necessary.					

Continued

	Current performance level				
Skills description	1	2	3	4	5
Political sensitivity – understands agendas and perspectives of others, recognises and balances needs of the group and the broader organisation					
Self awareness – recognises own temperament, skills and motivations and their impact on performance on self and others					
Visioning – Has the ability to provide inspiration by focussing on the 'big picture' and future possibilities					

Note: A fuller version of this questionnaire, AIMS: The Emotional Element is available from Ashridge.

Now analyse your responses to each of the items in the questionnaire and list those skills that appear to be:

Strengths..
....
....
....
....
....

Areas for development..
....
....
....
....
....

Weaknesses..
....
....
....
....
....

Some of the other questions we asked in our survey are detailed below and the responses to these questions have been used to inform the contents of this book, various articles and the continued development of our training programme. *Influencing Strategies and Skills.*

The table below indicates the responses given by the respondents to three further questions in our questionnaire.

What are your own particular influencing strengths?	What skills do you want to develop to be a more effective influencer?	Think of a situation where you have failed to influence others – why do you think you have failed?
1. Communication skills	1. Communication skills	1. Lack of preparation
2. Listening	2. Influencing styles	2. Poor style
3. Knowledge	3. Process of influencing	3. Lack of viable solution to problem
4. Motivation	4. Preparation	4. Inability to engage others
5. Empathy	5. Self confidence	5. Lack of understanding of context
6. Tailoring message	6. Credibility	6. No credibility
7. Persistence	7. Empathy	7. Low self confidence
8. Personality	8. Emotional detachment	8. Lack of conviction on argument
9. Expertise	9. Conflict management	9. Lack of knowledge
10. Leadership skills	10. Planning	10. Poor argument

Having assessed yourself against each of the skills what follows are brief descriptions of all the core skills – what they involve and ideas on how you can improve your skills in the area. It is also important to recognise that many of these skills and attitudes overlap and affect one another. For instance, demonstrating excellent awareness of others' needs will also relate to aspects of communication skills. Very few of the skills or attitudes can be looked at in isolation as there is a significant degree of inter-relationship between them all.

Communication skills

This whole area can be broken down into a range of key skills:

Listening   is the key skill and people who lack ability in this area simply cannot call themselves influencers. Listening is one of those skills that we acquire – it tends not to be taught – unlike many other key skills. So, how do we learn to listen effectively? Many people feel they do not and therefore see it as one of their weaknesses. If we had a pound for every time an individual on one of our programmes has identified listening as one of their development needs we would be wealthy indeed.

> It is the province of knowledge to speak and it is the privilege of wisdom to listen

Oliver Wendell Holmes (1809–1894)

Listening is a complex two way process involving a range of communication skills. It involves both receiving information and transmitting it. While we are listening we are noticing not only the words and vocal tones of the speaker, but seeing their behaviour – their facial expression, gestures and many other non-verbal clues. We are also evaluating our perceptions of the feeling they are conveying – all of this leads to our interpretation of the message that is being conveyed. But then, while we are receiving information we are also transmitting information. All of this information will have an effect upon the speaker and of course on the listener in terms of how the data is received. So what are we transmitting while listening? As a listener our non-verbal behaviour may be indicating all sorts of messages to the speaker. For instance; agreement, puzzlement, disagreement, boredom, excitement – all of which will have an effect upon the speaker and what they are saying.

> The tendency to react to any emotionally meaningful statement by forming an evaluation of it from our own perspective is – the major barrier to interpersonal communication.

Carl Rogers

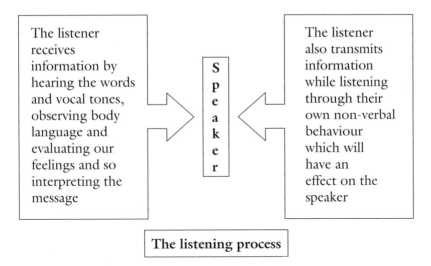

| The listener receives information by hearing the words and vocal tones, observing body language and evaluating our feelings and so interpreting the message | S p e a k e r | The listener also transmits information while listening through their own non-verbal behaviour which will have an effect on the speaker |

The listening process

How we listen is often an unknown to us. For instance, we remember the participant who came on one of our programmes and clearly identified one of his key development needs was to develop his listening skills (among other things!). Well, it wasn't difficult to see why. Early on in the course we did a short group exercise where we recorded onto video tape the group discussing a topic and attempting to reach a decision. Pretty quickly we noticed something a bit unusual about this chap – he appeared to close his eyes a lot when not talking yet he appeared to be following all that was being said as his interjections and comments were often spot on and adding value to the conversation. However, as an observer of the exercise it was difficult for me to do anything other than observe – we were not players in the discussion therefore we did not know how it felt to be at the receiving end of this behaviour – we could hazard a guess but certainly could not authentically share with him how this made me feel. Fortunately we had the video and five others who took part to help in this process.

Initially we had a group discussion about the process and behaviours of the group members and our participant found it hard to accept some of the feedback he received, most of which was not positive. Though, we all recognised that much of what he had contributed was sensible, the body language was seen as so 'off putting' that the other people in the group were quite negative about his contribution. However, when watching the video he too was quite critical of his behaviour and at last he understood why so many people thought him a poor listener.

This of course was a fairly extreme case; most people's listening problems are not so obvious. Some of the main problems we observe are:

▶ Interrupting – cutting in on another person without allowing them to finish their speech
▶ Responding without checking understanding

▶ Reactions to a particular type of person or their way of communicating
▶ Distractions – other things going on around you
▶ Prejudice – something about the person, for instance: accent or hair colour
▶ Lack of interest in the subject

In general many of us do find it difficult to be truly effective listeners so how can we improve our ability in this very important skill? First of all stop talking! Bite your tongue, count to ten, be silent and listen. While you are listening, demonstrate that you are interested by maintaining a good level of eye contact with the speaker/s, using supportive body language such as head nods and sounds like mmm, ok, etc. Don't look at your Emails, answer the telephone or doodle. It is also helpful to observe the speakers body language and vocal usage – so many cues and clues about feelings and intentions are suggested not only by the words used but also by the way they are said and what the person is doing as they talk.

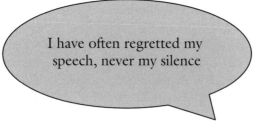

I have often regretted my speech, never my silence

Xenocrates 396–314 BC

For instance, when someone is talking in an animated and speedy way, with supportive hand and arm gestures and a positive open facial expression you can probably safely assume they have a strongly positive feeling about the topic. On the other hand, if they are reticent and more thoughtful, perhaps with short pauses to think, accompanied by upward eye movements, then this may indicate less confidence in or knowledge of the topic.

The important thing in communication is to hear what isn't being said.

Peter Drucker

The important thing when interpreting messages in this way is to be reasonably familiar with the person and thus have some knowledge of their
typical vocal usage and body language.

It might also be useful to put yourself in the others person's shoes –
imagine their viewpoint and perspective. Stop yourself interrupting, it's
too easy when you don't agree with someone or thing to interrupt and
put your own point of view across – as Stephen Covey (2004) says 'Seek
first to understand and then to be understood'. By this we mean let the
person finish what they are saying then test your understanding by summarising and questioning. Practise rephrasing – which involves repeating
to the speaker what you have heard and understood but in your words
not theirs. This is a key skill for demonstrating that you have listened to
them – not necessarily agreed but listened all the same.

In our experience and when influencing in general we find that what
people want is the opportunity to be listened to and understood not necessarily agreed with although this is pleasant too.

Questioning and probing is the ability to ask the right question at
the right time and it is the hall-mark of a good influencer. The natural
tendency of many influencers is to talk too much. This results in leading
the influencee to the influencer's way of thinking and thus limiting the
ability of the discussion to reach a mutually successful outcome. A truly
effective influencer not only advocates his own views but also uses questions to inquire about the other party's perspectives on the issue under
discussion. At the very simplest level there are two basic types of question:

▶ **The open question** to which there are many possible answers, for
   instance, 'What are your views about …?'
   and
▶ **The closed question** to which you require a specific answer, for
   instance, 'Do you agree?'

Both open and closed questions should be used in the process of
influencing – open ones to explore the issue fully and closed ones to
check facts and control the discussion.

Open questions can be further subdivided into:

The probe question, which is used to

▶ show interest or encouragement
▶ seek further information
▶ explore detail
▶ demonstrate understanding
▶ regain control

For instance, 'What makes you say that?' and 'Why do you think that?'

Probing involves asking linked questions in order to drill deeper and deeper into an issue and is important in influencing when getting the full picture is vital. A useful technique to develop or practise is the concept of funnelling which involves using an open question to begin a discussion on a particular topic then follow on with probe questions in order to explore the topic fully.

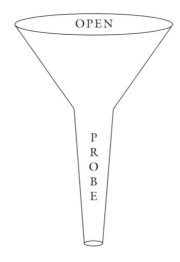

The clarification question, which is used to test your understanding of the issue, for instance, 'So, what you are saying is...?' and 'Let me see if I understand, ...?'

A truly effective question is one that encourages people to answer freely and honestly. An ineffective question is one which inhibits people and manipulates or distorts the information or outcome in some way.

To ensure effective questioning you should:

▶ phrase questions positively
▶ use language the other parties are comfortable with
▶ focus on one topic at a time
▶ be short and to the point – avoid rambling
▶ demonstrate genuine interest
▶ show that you are listening by demonstrating understanding

EXAMPLE

When Nigel Melville was Director of Rugby at Wasps – one of the UK's top rugby clubs, he wasn't convinced that having the goal of wanting to win the League served much purpose. Yes it demonstrated the players' ambition. But he wanted to know what he could do to make that goal come to life, something they could touch now, not waiting to lift a piece of silverware in nine months. He didn't want their goal to be thrown back in their faces, he wanted them to explore it in greater detail. So he called a meeting and asked a range of questions:

▶ **If we were to lift the Trophy what would it take?**
▶ **What would we have to achieve during the season?**
▶ **How many games would we have to win?**
▶ **Could we differentiate between winning at home and away?**
▶ **What would we have to do now to generate the required momentum?**
▶ **What would the key ingredients be?**
▶ **How fit /strong/quick/skilful/physical/committed do we need to be?**
▶ **How would we eat/drink/sleep/travel/socialise/celebrate and handle the media?**
▶ **How would we play? What style? What patterns? What calls?**

During this meeting the questioning went on and on. The team began to develop what they needed to do to win the League.

Awareness of body language – yours and theirs. This means being aware of the non verbal messages you are projecting to others, and ensuring that your words and body language are synchronised in order to give a congruent message. You should also develop the skill to read others' body language assessing what they are 'saying' in their non verbal messages and being responsive to these messages.

Body language consists of a rich combination of postures, movements, gestures and messages conveyed through dress. One's look and appearance says a lot about a person – for instance, if you wear a uniform like a nurse or policeman this says something about you; your hairstyle, your clothes, your shoes, your jewellery and everything else about you conveys a message to others. This whole area can prove to be very difficult to read in today's much more casual business life. Gone are the days of the business suit, a white shirt and a blue tie. Now we are faced with dress down Friday and casual dress as a matter of course. So what do we read into the

Managing Director who wears jeans and a tee shirt to the office, or the team member who wears a nose stud, or the junior clerk who always wears a business suit. Undoubtedly all these modes of attire say something about us and in turn are interpreted by others in ways known only to them. The important thing here is to be aware that what you wear, how you wear it and how you look is all part of your impression management strategy.

The postures and gestures one uses are also open to interpretation; for instance, the way you sit and the hand and arm gestures you use. If you sit in a slouched way this may convey certain messages which are different to when you sit up straight. Varying your postures and gestures and using appropriate body language can help you influence a situation. For instance, in a meeting by using posture and gesture movements you can convey different messages, for example sitting back in your chair with hands and arms relaxed still conveys listening behaviour, sitting forward and gesticulating with your arms and hands may indicate a need to speak.

Nearness and orientation is an interesting aspect of body language. A small touch on the shoulder, a kiss on the cheek when greeting someone, distance from the other person, whether you are face to face, or across a desk, or free from barriers, or leaning towards, or leaning away from, all these aspects of non-verbal communication are contributing to the impact you have on others and your impression management. Nearness can indicate an intensity or perhaps intimacy in a relationship. Spatial awareness is an important aspect of non-verbal behaviour especially when meeting someone for the first time. We all have a personal space preference and that preference can depend upon who we are communicating with. Psychologists have found that there are four zones of preference:

Intimate – up to about 18 inches apart and usually reserved for those people with whom we have a close relationship and typically used when we are discussing something quite personal and intimate

Personal – about 2/3 feet – this one is used in more open social settings again with people to whom we are quite close

Social – about 4 to 6 feet – most of us are relatively comfortable at this distance when interacting with people who we have recently met or who we don't know very well

Public – about 12 feet – this is the distance we tend to feel comfortable with when talking with people we don't know for instance in a presentation type setting.

When you meet someone for the first time the distance at which they stand from you can help indicate their comfort with you and the conversation. Of course it can always mean something else, for instance, in some cultures it is inappropriate to get too close to people unless they are close family members. Fiona will always remember her early days in England; having moved from a small village in Scotland she found it quite unsettling and overly intimate when some of her new English girlfriends (same gender) hugged and kissed her when they met each other, in say a restaurant or other social setting. This had not been the way where she was brought up and it has taken many years for her to feel comfortable with this common social practice. One of our business school colleagues – a British man – lived in Africa for some time .His next door neighbour liked to have a chat over the garden fence. This also happens in the UK. The difference here was that his neighbour – a local man – held our colleague's hand during the conversation.

Facial Expression, small movements of the face, for instance, eye brow movements, smiles, grimaces, blushing etc. all convey messages to others. So many feelings can be expressed by simple variations in facial movement – sadness, anger, surprise, fear, happiness to name a few. When interacting with others perhaps the most impactful and positive facial expression is the use of the smile. The smile usually indicates a degree of interest and happiness at taking part in the communication and will certainly indicate a willingness to listen. However, one must also be aware that it is extremely easy to fake one's facial expression or to learn to use one's face to convey false feelings. For instance, have you ever watched a television award ceremony? When the award is announced obviously you see the smiling happy winner and then very quickly the camera will move to show you the various losers – it is rare that they are doing anything else other than smiling and clapping – I wouldn't mind betting that this is not demonstrating a true reflection of their feelings!

So, as with so much of body language ones facial expression can be used to convey the important messages you choose to convey not always what you are feeling. Awareness is the key here – awareness of the signals you transmit with your various facial expressions. Are they appropriate for the conversation you are having at the time and most importantly are they conveying the message you wish to convey?

Perhaps the most important messages of all are gained from eye contact and the ability to engage in and maintain eye contact in an effective manner. Adopting the appropriate gaze level with people during conversation in order to convey messages like sincerity, interest and empathy is important for effective influencing. People who find it difficult to gain and maintain eye contact can be regarded suspiciously by others, while those who find it easy to do so are more likely to be regarded as confident, knowledgeable and in control.

Body language is a powerful form of communication and undoubtedly has an effect on the messages one conveys. The most important aspect of body language is to ensure that it is synchronised with the words and paralanguage being used. Reading body language is a skill in itself. Looking for clusters of non-verbal behaviour and regular usage of expressions, gestures etc. together with how these relate to the words and topic under discussion is probably more important than overly concentrating on single gestures and expressions. Clusters and regularity may then be regarded as aspects of an individual's communication process all of which will contribute to the messages you are conveying to others. This of course makes it difficult to be sure of the true meaning of the messages being conveyed when we are dealing with people we don't know very well.

The possibilities for abuse of body language are enormous and it is always possible to manipulate situations by clever use of body language which can be dangerous and misleading.

Another key area is to be able to listen to how something is said and not just what is said. According to one source, 93 per cent of all communication is non-verbal skill (Mehrabian, 1977) In particular, this research highlighted that this was the case when people talk about their emotions. If we accept that influencing so often involves a range of different emotions then this highlights the importance of all aspects of non-verbal communication and the need to consider this as part of the whole process.

Language and paralanguage – we know that words are only one aspect of communication, but in certain contexts words have much more meaning than the 7 per cent that Mehrabian attributes to them. We believe that Mehrabian has underestimated the importance of the words that you choose. One researcher in this area, Birdwhistle (1999) recognised that non-verbal Communication counted for more than 65 per cent of the meaning of the interaction. Therefore it is tremendously important for you to be aware of the different aspects of non-verbal Communication. However, this still leaves a large chunk of meaning imparted by the words you choose.

The percentage varies according to the context. We saw above that the percentage in the average one to one conversation is 65/35. In some situations, for example, a briefing to a reporter in a war zone on personal safety, that percentage is probably going to be more like 90 per cent words and 10 per cent non-verbal.

So your words should have an impact – they need to awaken the listeners or readers interest. Choose words that are colourful, look for metaphors that paint a visual picture. Appeal to all the senses.

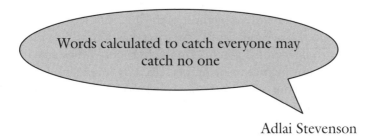

Words calculated to catch everyone may catch no one

Adlai Stevenson

In Neuro Linguistic Programming we learn to use words that respond to the three sub-modalites of visual/auditory/kinaesthetic. Visual people are those who tend to relate to language containing visual words, for example 'let me paint you a picture...' or 'imagine this scene...'. Auditory thinking people respond to phrases like 'I like the sound of that...' or 'I hear what you are getting at...'. Kinaesthetic thinking people relate to feeling and touch and will use phrases like 'I like the feel of this...' or 'Things seem to be going smoothly on this one'. In particular it is important to notice which sense is predominant in an individual's language and appeal to that one in order to create better rapport.

Positive is more effective than negative – you want to hear the positive benefits of what you are proposing. You need to pay attention to the tone of voice used. Most people have too little control over which tone they use – for instance, an aggressive tone is met by defensiveness, and a sneering, patronising tone will not make you a great influencer. You need to know when to be firm and when to give way. Paralanguage is about more than tone, it's also about timing and pace, volume, use of silence, the use of interjections (mmm..., yes, head nods and shakes etc.) and accent. Slight changes in speed, intonation and volume can alter the meaning of a sentence. For instance, one can indicate enthusiasm for a topic by changing pace, volume and intonation by heightening the emphasis on certain words. Psychologically many of us are intuitively aware when someone is attempting to convince us of something that they themselves have not bought into – we give ourselves away not by what we are saying but by the way we are saying it and what we are doing when we say it unless of course the speaker is an exceptionally good actor.

A recent article by Caroline MacLeod in *The Scotsman* (December 2005) reported on the importance of accents in communication. So the accent you have may even have an effect on how influential you are. A Report by UK communications consultancy Aziz Corporation says that among business people there is prejudice against strong English regional accents.

In business, people with a Home Counties accent are considered to be generally successful, followed by those with American accents followed by those with Scottish accents. In the survey it was found that there was a belief that strong regional accents from Liverpool, Wales and the West Country were not helpful in being perceived as successful. Clearly how someone regards your accent is rather subjective. Nevertheless it is interesting to reflect on the impact that your accent might have on others. Clearly it might be difficult for a non British person to distinguish between British accents, and it is more likely that people from your own country would be the most judgemental.

In Germany though, the same thing exists – we are told that the Saxon accent is considered inferior to other accents. There are preconceptions, for example, many people (even in Scotland) tend to associate a Glaswegian accent with being rather tough! We find that a Scottish accent can often sound rather harsh to the ears of our English colleagues! On the other hand many call centres are based in Scotland because the people answering the phone are considered to be trustworthy.

In any case most people will have a range of accents they can use – from strong regional accent through to 'Received Pronunciation'. Being flexible and adapting your accent (perhaps softening it a little) to the context is key.

The questions to ask are:

▶ How strong is your accent?
▶ How suited is it to the environment in which you are operating?
▶ How much flexibility do you have? In other words are you able to modify your accent at will, or are you a prisoner of that accent?
▶ To what extent do you match the vocabulary of your listeners?

We have seen many managers whose influencing ability is increased by their regional accents. When the accent is perceived favourably and when it is clear and understandable, then we think that it is an asset. However we have also met managers who have strong accents that are rather difficult to understand, especially in an international context, and who have little or no flexibility in their ability to modify that accent.

Verbal fluency – the ability to put forward a clear and lucid case with confidence and flair is a major benefit for any influencer. Skill in this area not only demonstrates knowledge of the issue but if executed properly it can also show commitment, enthusiasm and level of involvement in the issue under discussion. Use of sophisticated techniques such as metaphor, analogy and visioning can all help in this area. In addition there is a very close link to awareness of body language; how you use your voice and non-verbals to assist in getting your message across is all part of verbal fluency. Choosing words carefully and with the receiver in mind, avoiding the use of negative statements and expressing yourself in an authentic and genuine manner all contribute to your verbal fluency.

Awareness of others' needs

Awareness of others' needs demands a range of different skills and attitudes and perhaps the most important of these is *empathy* which is about having the ability to understand and identify the other person's feelings, ideas and circumstances. Putting yourself onto the same wavelength as others so that you can relate to them at an emotional level involves using both your heart and head. Many people have an innate ability in this area; others have to work hard at it. Much is down to preparation and knowing the people you are trying to influence. By putting yourself into their shoes and asking yourself some searching questions you can begin to analyse where the other person is coming from and what is affecting their perspective about the issue under discussion. By showing others that you understand their perspective you are demonstrating empathy.

Empathy also requires sincerity to be truly effective. Demonstrating sincerity leads to trust in a relationship and it is through trust that effective influencing relationships grow. Openness, genuineness and authenticity all contribute towards sincerity. Demonstrating sincerity requires one to be self aware and to understand the messages you are conveying through your words, paralanguage and body language. If you feel you cannot trust the person attempting to influence you then the likelihood of success is limited. Showing *sensitivity* through understanding and compassion also demonstrates concern for others' needs and is important for true empathy to be felt.

I try to understand the concerns and motivations of others. If I was them what would influence me?

Participant, Ashridge
Influencing Strategies and Skills Programme

Building rapport with others is about getting onto the same wavelength as those you are attempting to influence; making the right connections and developing the ability to empathise indicate good influencing behaviour. It is a key skill and if you cannot develop rapport with others you are unlikely to be an effective influencer and your influencing approach will be restricted to the use of power and authority. Rapport building demands you to focus on and pay attention to the people you are influencing in order to develop a comfortable and natural way of communicating with them.

So how can you develop rapport? There are many ways, one of the basic ones is to be a good listener (see earlier), be interested in what other people have to say, don't interrupt, don't finish their thoughts for them, be patient, observe what they say, how they say it and what they do as they talk.

Pacing A technique from Neuro Linguistic Programming which is a good way of building rapport or demonstrating empathy. This involves going with their flow so to speak and thus avoiding any glaring mismatches between your body language and theirs and your tone of voice and theirs. For example, if you speak very loudly and quickly and are trying to influence someone who speaks slowly, carefully and softly the mismatch is very obvious. The answer is to slow down, speak more softly. However it is important to regulate rather than imitate. If you are very tall and influencing someone who is much shorter then bend down a bit, or sit down, don't stand next to them and overpower them. It's similar to when you are talking to a child – you crouch down to their level.

A warning though, this is not so much about matching as it is about avoiding mismatching. In matching you are told to mirror the others person's behaviour, but we find this can be difficult to do well and can easily be counter productive. It can easily end up being seen as mimicking rather than pacing or matching.

Adaptability

Adaptability is largely about your own ability to change and to react to the situation appropriately. The ability to flex and change your approach, style and behaviour will help you appeal to as wide an audience as possible. This together with an openness of mind such that you are willing to listen and understand other people's perspectives will indicate adaptability.

An inability to be adaptable can be seen as belligerence and can lead to being regarded as one who cannot be influenced, as we have already

> Whoever desires constant success
> must change his conduct with the times

Nicolo Machiavelli (1469–1527)

established influencing is a two way process – if you want to influence others you must also be open to influence yourself. Receptiveness to listening and taking on board the ideas of others demonstrates adaptability.

Change is a fact of life for all of us. Influencing is all about change therefore it follows that demonstrating adaptability and flexibility signals an openness to change. And, actually showing people that you are flexible and adaptable will set you apart from the mediocre influencers. Many people get anchored in their own preferred ways of influencing and therefore get stuck when they encounter people who respond to a different approach or style. By understanding your own typical approach (see Influencing Style questionnaire in Chapter 4) and then developing skills and approaches relevant to other styles you will broaden your repertoire of influencing behaviour and thus your ability to adapt to others' needs.

In addition to skill development you will also need to develop antennae for recognising when you need to adapt. The previous section on awareness of others' needs should help with ideas on this.

Conflict

The ability to effectively deal with conflict by confronting the issue rather than blaming and finger pointing is important for so many influencing discussions. As influencing so very often involves people discussing an issue from different perspectives this can lead to disagreement. So, the ability to successfully manage potential conflict situations is vital for successful and effective influencing outcomes. One of the most important aspects of conflict management is the ability to manage one's own emotional response to people's differing perspectives on an issue.

Often when you enter an influencing discussion you encounter different opinions which will involve you in emotion management. Sometimes our initial response might be to disagree and get angry with the other person. This sort of response will tend not to be terribly influential and indeed will tend to have the effect of turning the other off so making influencing impossible. You may also wish to manage or control your emotions and responses to appear impassive to the issue under discussion so as not to give your thoughts away.

When faced with conflicting views on an issue where influencing the way ahead is important it is best to be tough on the issues but caring about the relationship. By this we mean developing the capability to question, explore and fully investigate the issue but remaining neutral to the people involved. What you are doing is demonstrating a genuine interest in the people, the issue and their views and therefore less likely to become involved in conflict.

This can also contribute to one's ability to compromise. By entering into a dialogue and fully exploring and understanding all perspectives of the issue under discussion it makes it easier to collaborate. You can build on each other's ideas and ultimately reach a workable compromise.

Impact

This is about being aware of the impact and impression you create with people, when you first meet them, as you develop your relationship and indeed in long term relationships. The impact you create in various situations will undoubtedly have an effect upon the way people relate to you. So, for instance do you exude confidence and self assurance on first meeting people, or are you more likely to be more reticent and reserved? Neither one is right or wrong, simply different; however, both will have an impact on the way the people you are interacting with regard you and therefore will affect your relationship going ahead. So understanding and managing the impact you create in various situations is a key component of effective influencing.

Tempering the physical presence – if you are 6′2″, 220lbs and have a deep loud(ish) northern accent – how do you make sure the 'little guys' are confident enough to tell you that you might have it wrong.

Participant, Ashridge
Influencing Strategies and Skills Programme

First impressions are often lasting and therefore have a major role to play in developing an influencing relationship. But, it's not only first impressions, it's those lasting impressions people are left with when they have interacted with you or worked with you for any length of time. Successful and effective influencers are very aware of the impact and impression they create and manage this very carefully. This may seem rather manipulative, but like many aspects of interpersonal behaviour it's all about the outcome you desire. Yes it might be manipulative if you are purposely behaving in such a way that the people you are influencing will be losers, for instance, if you have a strong belief in an issue that you know others may find difficult to go along with, yet you adopt a positive, confident and knowledgeable stance on it. And, by putting an unbalanced case, for instance, focussing mainly on the positive aspects and thus convincing them that your suggestion is the only way ahead without sharing the downsides in full, you would certainly be manipulating your audience. Therefore, their first impression of you may have been very positive but probably the lasting impression will be that they will be more wary of working with you and listening to you in the future.

Some people find impression management comes very naturally and others are less comfortable with it. The important issue is to be aware of the impact you are creating on a day to day basis. So, it might be worth asking some of your colleagues to describe the impact you have on them. This might help you to understand how you come across to different people. It is also important to recognise that this is a complex area and what has positive impact on one person may have a less positive impact on another.

Exercise

Try this brief experiment:

Identify someone in the public eye that is universally liked yet there is something about that person that you do not like and you feel you do not trust them. Think about it, what is it you dislike, what gives you this impression.

This highlights that as with many aspects of influencing this area is highly subjective. The main issue to be aware of is the impact you are creating – plan it, think it through and vary your behaviour for different situations and scenarios. This should not cause you to have to act, but simply to vary your behaviour to suit the situation, people and issue under discussion. Demonstrate consistency, not necessarily in approach but in *behaviour and personality*, in order to gain credibility with others.

Networking

Networking is all about relationship building both within and outside one's organisation. Each one of us has an influencing network – those people with whom we interact on a regular basis. Typically this will be people whom we are familiar with and who come into contact with us frequently. Good networking involves constantly widening this group to develop relationships with a broad range of people who can help, support and add value.

Some of the people in our network are exceedingly well known to us and can be regarded as close colleagues or friends. These are the people we have to influence on a regular basis and we will be familiar with their way of operating. Others are less well known and really fit the description of acquaintances. The important thing in all of this is to continue to develop new relationships.

Throughout our life networks will change, some people will remain constant, while others will come and go. Good networking involves you in being self aware, understanding your organisation, the issues you are involved in and your plans – current and future. Awareness in these areas will enable you to recognise and develop appropriate relationships at appropriate times in your life. On the face of it this sounds a bit manipulative, i.e. developing relationships just because they might be of use to you! Remember networking involves relationship building and this also is a two way process; people always have the choice whether or not to work with and relate to you. Like most other aspects of influencing building trust and respect are vital for successful networking and if you betray that trust you may think you have a good network of contacts but when you try to leverage your network they simply don't play the game.

Building and developing your network involves hard yet enjoyable work as typically people want mutuality in any relationship.

Personal approach

Personal approach is all about the characteristics of your particular approach to influencing. Obviously we will all develop our own influencing personality, however there are certain characteristics that are particularly beneficial for effectiveness.

Patience is not only a virtue but also a necessity where influencing is concerned! Influencing does not just happen overnight, it is a long-term process. Where people and their emotions are involved, time and timing must also play a part.

As influencing is usually a long-term process, developing a trusting atmosphere and relationship with those you are influencing is key to success. We have all been manipulated by others at some time in our lives and no doubt remember how that felt! Trusting someone who has manipulated you in the past may not be easy. A good example of this is shown in Shakespeare's *Henry V* where after persuading the citizens of Harfleur to yield, Henry exhorts his commander, the Duke of Exeter to treat them with mercy. '*Come Uncle Exeter, Go you and enter Harfleur, There remain and fortify it strongly against the French; Use mercy to them all.*' (*Henry V*, by William Shakespeare). He knows that if he does not carry out his word he will not be able to use the same strategy in the future.

Being credible is about your reputation and how you have developed this within your personal networks. Our reputations are often based on perception and how we deal with others in a wide range of situations. Personal credibility and track record are therefore vital for gaining people's interest and trust.

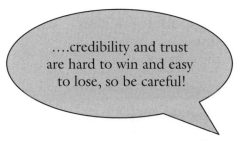

....credibility and trust are hard to win and easy to lose, so be careful!

Nigel Melville – Rugby Coach

Having the courage to speak up for your own ideas and beliefs involves taking risks – often calculated risks in terms of trying out new ideas and approaches. Clearly this involves knowing your stuff, doing your homework and paving the way with others – in fact planning and preparation.

Demonstrating enthusiasm for and belief in your topic or issue is vital because if you can't then how will you manage to convince others about it. Enthusiasm, however, is demonstrated in a variety of ways. At one end of the scale is full on passion for the topic and at the other is absolute commitment – both are demonstrated by the choice of words, paralanguage and body language – the difference is in the energy during the delivery. Passion is usually accompanied by significant levels of energy, while commitment is perhaps less visibly energetic yet no less enthusiastic.

Persuasiveness

Persuasiveness is all about having a convincing way with others. It's about recognising and anticipating alternative points of view. Anticipation is the key here; this allows you to prepare in advance for differences of opinion. Showing people that you are willing to listen to others' perspectives on an issue, and even that you have already thought about them can be immensely convincing when attempting to influence others. Giving thought to alternative viewpoints means that you will have looked at the issue from a more rounded perspective than simply going with your own original ideas. It can force you to ask yourself questions and reflect on the issue prior to entering into discussion with others, thus ensuring that you are well prepared for whatever challenges, questions and barriers you encounter.

Influencing almost always involves change of some sort or another, those people with good persuasive skills will understand resistance, what causes it and how to overcome it. Typically resistance to change is for one of the following reasons:

▶ Conflicting loyalties, beliefs, values or attitudes
▶ General apathy or scepticism
▶ Negative views of you the influencer
▶ Fear of the unknown
▶ Lack of information or misinformation
▶ Reluctance to experiment or risk aversion
▶ Threat to core skills, competences, status or earnings

Resistance is a normal human reaction to change of any kind and frequently it is due to a failure to find the right way to communicate the desired message. The successful and effective influencer will recognise that in order to lower the resistance and break through it the message has to be delivered in a different way. So, identifying the reason for the resistance is essential and will enable you to plan the most effective influencing process.

Persuasion is often more effective than force

Aesop (620–560 BC)

To be truly persuasive you must put forward your ideas with conviction and enthusiasm and be able to win the support of others by involvement and participation. Although you may have a sound argument how forcefully and with what conviction do you present it? A poor argument with great delivery may not be enough but a great argument delivered in a flat, monotonous voice with no enthusiasm or conviction certainly will not be enough. At Ashridge we meet many managers who have simply never thought about their delivery, never asked for feedback on how they sound and what their impact is. You need to think about how you sound, how you stress key parts of your presentation, how enthusiastic you sound. If you don't sound convinced how can you expect others to be? As we pointed out earlier Mehrabian's research indicates that 33 per cent of meaning is through paralinguistics – the way you speak.

So how much conviction do you carry when you are trying to influence? We worked with some senior managers in a multinational energy company recently. We asked them to work on a change initiative they were currently addressing, and to do some work on how they might go about getting buy in for the initiative. All the managers did a great job of analysing the situation and presenting it logically. What was lacking though, was enthusiasm, conviction, emotion and energy.

This is reflected in many presentations that we see in organisations from Board room down to shop floor. The argument is presented in a flat, boring way, with no connection to the needs of the listeners, little conviction, even less passion! Try listening to the great orators – Churchill, Martin Luther King, JFK, Nelson Mandela – listen to how they speak, listen to the passion and conviction. We are not asking you to become a classic orator, just to learn how to put some passion, enthusiasm and conviction into your words. The best place to start is to really believe in what you are saying. If you don't – for example when you have to interpret and present others' perspectives for instance the senior management's position on an issue – analyse the content and find out what you DO believe. Build on that and inject some passion. You don't have to agree with everything, but if you believe in nothing at all in a position, then it's unlikely that you will be able to influence effectively. It also means that you should probably try to go back to senior management and discuss putting something in there that you do believe in. If that fails then you need to consider your effectiveness in that role.

One way of looking at this is to try and find a meta perspective. You may not agree with everything that is being asked, but if you don't agree with the how then maybe you can believe in the what. George Prince in his book *The Practise of Creativity*, describes an interesting methodology. Often when we are in discussion we adopt an adversarial position right from the start. Someone says, 'I think we should do x', then another person in the meeting says, 'No that won't work', or 'That's stupid', or 'that's a crazy idea'. You in turn say, 'No I disagree, My idea is better'. So you get in to a downward negative spiral which is not helpful to resolving the issue you have to tackle.

Prince suggests that you are rarely completely wrong, so your ideas should not be rubbished or dismissed – and very rarely completely right. His solution is to take the point of the other persons idea that you *do* like, and say something like – 'What I like about your thinking is …'! So, you focus on the positive aspects of the idea, rather than concentrating solely (as we so often do) on the negative.

Political sensitivity

This involves a degree of astuteness and awareness about people and processes in your organisation or influencing environment. Politically skilled people seem to have an innate ability to know precisely what to do in the many different social situations they experience at work. Knowing and being able to identify key stakeholders in various situations and understanding that alienating these key personnel can lead to creation of obstacles and barriers to success. By developing the sensitivity to approach people in appropriate ways, adapting and adjusting behaviours as necessary will lead to more likelihood of success.

Political sensitivity is a difficult skill to train and to some extent it reflects a degree of tacit knowledge which is acquired through experience and time. However, that said, awareness of self and others together with the recognition that one has to vary the approach, behaviour and style for different situations and people will go a long way to helping you to develop in this area. Political sensitivity is most necessary when one is 'going against the grain' or challenging the status quo in some way. Recognising that much influencing does involve change and challenge to be able to do it in a sensitive, respectful and effective way is highly beneficial. While political sensitivity and skill may appear manipulative it really is largely about reaching an effective outcome by recognising what needs to be done and understanding the most effective processes and behaviours to do so. Trust, diplomacy and respect are all key attributes of politically sensitive people and this means open and honest behaviour where the outcome is seen as a win-win.

Political skills need development. I do not suffer fools and in my view occasionally within an organisation you need to be willing to accept fools. Sometimes my drive and passion can be seen as negative, by others as 'gung ho' particularly in the industry I work, insurance which is very conservative.

Participant, Ashridge Influencing
Strategies and Skills Programme

Self awareness

Self knowledge – awareness of your own strengths, weaknesses, beliefs and values – is invaluable for effective influencing. This alone will often determine the approach you take and skills you use when attempting to influence others. This self knowledge must be tested and held up to the mirror. As Robert Burns wrote in his poem *To A Louse*,

O wad some Power the giftie gie us
To see oursels as others see us
It wad frae mony a blunder free us
An foolish notion

Now the English translation! Oh, would that some power give us the gift to see ourselves as others see us … .Self knowledge implies getting feedback from others on our approach and how we come across. Asking others for feedback can be a daunting experience – if you ask you never quite know what someone is going to say in response. However, without feedback how can we ever know how we are regarded by others?

In order to raise self awareness, feedback is vital to understand our strengths, weaknesses, and development needs and importantly to understand the impact of our behaviour on others. Simply asking someone for feedback often only elicits generalities at best or negative points at worst. For instance, we have observed that people often say 'fine' or 'the approach works for me' or something similar to this. This is pretty useless feedback as it tells you very little in relation to the actual skills and behaviours you are using. Also, if people only focus on the negative, for instance saying something like 'you come across as very opinionated' or 'you speak too quietly' or something similar then you are not getting balanced view of your behaviour.

We find that it is much more beneficial to ask for feedback about specific aspects of your influencing skills and behaviour, for instance:

▶ I'd be really grateful if you could observe my body language during this meeting and give me feedback on what you see me do and what works and doesn't for you.

or

▶ It would be really useful if during our discussion you would be willing to give me feedback relating to my skills as a listener.

By focussing the topic of the feedback you are much more likely to gain valuable data and to be able to enter into a dialogue with the person giving you the feedback to fully understand it. It is also important to consider who you ask to give you feedback. In our view trust and mutual respect are important characteristics of a feedback relationship, so make sure you carefully identify those people you ask.

Reflection can also be invaluable to raising your self awareness. Getting into the habit of self observation and reflection following discussions and dialogues can be highly beneficial to your self knowledge and understanding of your own skills and abilities. Many influencing relationships are with people you come into contact with on a regular basis. If you get into the habit of reviewing your performance each time you have interacted with them you should be able to build a picture of what works and what doesn't for the different characters you have to influence on a regular basis. This will also help you to realise where you have particular skill and where you need to develop new approaches and skills. A useful process for reflection is to take some time after important discussions/meetings to jot down notes about some or all of the following:

▶ What worked?
▶ What was difficult?
▶ What did you feel you did well?
▶ What could you have done better?
▶ How did the other/s react to you approach?
▶ What were your feelings during the interaction?
▶ What will you try differently next time you are in a similar situation? and
▶ What will you try next time you have to influence these people?

Visioning

Visioning in this context is about having the ability to look to the future and paint a picture of what could be, the outcomes you desire and being able to inspire others to buy into your vision or ideas. Visioning involves the use of exceptional communication skills: analogy, metaphor, symbolism, imagery, pictures and so on.

Visioning sounds terribly grand but we truly believe that all of us have the ability to present our vision – it's simply about sharing our dreams and thoughts of what could be in relation to our ideas. By suspending judgement and describing our dreams for the future we can often engage people at a different level in order to attract their attention and interest in exploring our ideas further.

No man that does not see visions will ever realise any high hope or undertake any high enterprise

Woodrow Wilson 1856–1924

Demonstrating enthusiasm in some way although not sufficient to influence, enthusiasm can often be the catalyst that gains others' attention and interest. If you are not enthusiastic about an issue about which you are attempting to influence others, why should they be?

So, for instance, let's imagine that you are one of a group of internal consultants attempting to bring about change following a merger or reorganisation. Part of the job at hand is to work with groups of people in the organisation to identify what is working well and what isn't. Now, you could simply organise a pretty straightforward discussion group where you encourage people to share ideas, and this might work and be all that is necessary. Or, you could be more bold and begin the discussion in a more creative way by establishing with the group why you are meeting with them and why it's important to be honest and share views openly – this might just have the effect of gaining more information and honest views. So, you could start your meetings with a short visioning statement probably assisted by an image or two on a power point presentation or flipchart. For instance:

'The way I currently see our organisation is a bit like a an oil tanker moving through the ocean very slowly and carefully, with any decisions to change direction being planned well in advance and then taking quite a time to execute. Business life today demands

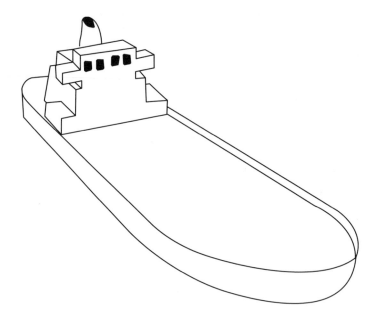

that we can no longer behave in this way, we must become more agile, creative and adaptable to change. So we must become more like sailing boats which are nimble and adapt and adjust to deal with the sea and winds that are constantly changing. Similarly we must develop the skill to be able to adapt and adjust to our business environment to meet the changing needs and to continue to grow and prosper. So what I need from you guys is ideas on what is and what isn't working in order to build our organisation of the future.'

A very simple vision that can engage people more emotionally to what you are trying to achieve. Also by using images and pictures you will very likely create a better understanding of what you want from your audience and what you stand for. After all they do say 'a picture paints a

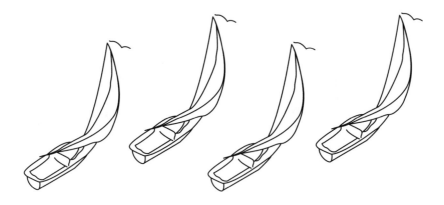

thousand words'! Visioning, of course need not always use the actual pictures – some of us are lucky enough to be able to paint pictures in the minds of others with the words and paralanguage we use. So, for instance many famous speeches illustrate this point. Martin Luther King perhaps is one good example when during the march on Washington for jobs and freedom in 1963 he said as part of a much longer speech (much of which was sharing his vision for the future): 'I have a dream that my four little children will one day live in a nation where they will not be judged by the color of their skin but by the content of their character.' A powerful statement (together with many others in the same speech) that creates in our minds images that we can connect with and thus be influenced by.

King of course was very well known, but you don't need to be famous to be able to use visioning, you do however have to be a little creative, enthusiastic and have belief in whatever you are trying to influence others about. Without the belief and enthusiasm visioning will be a challenge.

These skills are not an exhaustive list – however they are in our view key skills that contribute to success and effectiveness as an influencer and thus are worthy of attention.

✎ SUMMARY OF KEY POINTS

The eleven key skills are:

- ☞ Adaptability – flexibility to adjust your approach, language and views to suit different influencing situations
- ☞ Awareness of others' needs – awareness of other people, their reactions, needs, motivators and style
- ☞ Communication skills – ability to convey ideas and information clearly and in a manner appropriate to the audience using the skills of listening, questioning, probing, awareness of body language, language, paralanguage and verbal fluency
- ☞ Conflict – dealing effectively with interpersonal tensions
- ☞ Impact – showing energy and commitment to making things happen, projecting confidence, a can-do attitude, exploring new options for the business and challenging the current way of operating
- ☞ Networking – managing relationships in order to effectively build networks
- ☞ Personal approach – your personal characteristics and how you apply them in an influencing context – patience, trust, credibility, courage and enthusiasm
- ☞ Persuasiveness – persuades and influences in a way that gains commitment tailoring approach when necessary
- ☞ Political sensitivity – understanding agendas and perspectives of others, recognising and balancing needs of the group and the broader organisation
- ☞ Self awareness – recognising own temperament, skills and motivations and their impact on performance of self and others
- ☞ Visioning – ability to provide inspiration by focussing on the 'big picture' and future possibilities

4 Influencing Style

Tough Guy, Best Friend, Bull in a China Shop or Idealist?

> *Articulacy, confidence, the ability to evoke enthusiasm in others in the pursuit of a common goal, and the ability to recognise the most effective influence style in a given situation – these are my goals.*
>
> Ashridge Participant Influencing Strategies and
> Skills Programme 2004

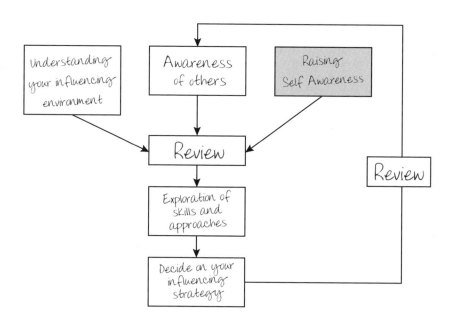

A MODEL FOR INFLUENCING

The approach used for influencing others will almost certainly have an impact on the outcome of any influencing discussion. Adopting the appropriate approach at the beginning of an influencing discussion can have a hugely beneficial effect upon the process and final outcome of the discussion. It is important that the person/s you are attempting to influence must feel that you wish to enter into a win-win relationship. Typically when influencing others we tend to have a preference in terms of the style we adopt. Sometimes this is an advantage:

▶ When influencing people we know they get what they expect
▶ Predictability
▶ Self confidence when using our preferred style at the start of the process and discussion
▶ Comfort with the approach

However, sticking to one tried and tested style or approach can have significant disadvantages:

▶ Adopting the wrong approach for all the people involved
▶ Turning people off at the first hurdle
▶ Giving the wrong messages to others in terms of your intentions from the style adopted
▶ Misjudging the situation or environment prevailing regarding the issue – for instance not taking into account others' emotions

The questionnaire that follows will help you to identify your preference and the style you feel most comfortable with and those you feel less comfortable with and even avoid.

INFLUENCING STYLE QUESTIONNAIRE

Examine the statements below and indicate in each horizontal line which approach you are most likely to use when influencing others and the approach you are least likely to use by putting either an M or an L in the column to the right of the appropriate statement. When you have completed your choice for each of the ten lines calculate your score for each column.

Apply pressure	State reasons for case	Encourage cooperative behaviour	Help people under-stand what could be
Competitive	Make recommendations	Demonstrates collaborative thinking	Inspire others
Confident in taking unpopular decisions	Willing to take a stand	Motivate by concensus building	Paint pictures of the future

Demanding	Recommend a way ahead	Get buy in from others	Provide inspiring messages when motivating
Motivated by the need to achieve goals	Recognised as an expert	Create rapport with others	Look for options, and new and stimulating ideas
Outspoken	Verbally fluent	Focus on all ideas collected – use 'we' statements	Expressive in presenting
Get impatient quickly	Put ideas forward with conviction	Value others' efforts	Use enthusiasm in presenting to others
Get straight to the point	Present in a focussed and concise manner	Seek the common ground	Present the big picture
Like to have the last word	Use logical argument to support case	Recognise the contribution of others	Articulate a vision of what might be
Put own point of view vigorously	Articulate in debate	Create an environment of openness and trust	Convey a sense of excitement
Total M's			
Total L's			

In the space below indicate which style you use most and which style you use least.

Directive	*Persuasive Reasoning*	*Collaborative*	*Visionary*

Note: The full version of the questionnaire together with supporting material is obtainable from Ashridge.

Having completed the questionnaire you now have a general idea of the style you use most frequently and therefore possibly the style you feel most comfortable using and the style you least use and therefore possibly use least effectively.

We believe that we very often overly depend upon one style and therefore develop the skills for this style to the detriment of the other approaches. To be truly effective as an influencer one should be using a range of styles to suit the topic, the people involved and the situation prevailing at the time.

Now that you have a better idea of the style you depend on most frequently you can also identify those styles you may have to develop for greater success and effectiveness. The information that follows gives details and descriptions of the four styles and should give you a good indication of what you can do to develop your skills in any of the underutilised styles.

Influencing styles

Influencing styles can be mapped in a number of ways. At a very general level there are two predominant styles – Push and Pull.

The *Push* approach is when you are directive, strong and powerful, when you can be clear and firm about your proposals. When using this style people tend to be very clear about where they want to go and the outcome they desire. The style involves more advocacy and telling and is often used when one is an expert or has a track record or history of success in a certain area. There are advantages in using this style; it is usually quick, focussed and very clear, however it also has certain disadvantages – predominantly that it can appear aggressive, uninvolving and arrogant.

When using the *Push* style, typically the key stages one goes through are:

▶ Setting the scene, identifying the problem you are attempting to solve and then making the proposal for the solution
▶ Invite reactions and comments
▶ Summarise what has been said
▶ Establish that everyone understands one another
▶ Deal with any objections either through persuasion or authority depending on whether you want commitment or compliance.
▶ Agree on the detail and who is going to do what

The *Pull* approach is one that depends upon using involving behaviours where your aim is to reach a joint agreement with others. In particular this approach is necessary when you require long-term commitment to the outcome. It is the complete opposite of the *Push* style. In using it people use supportive, encouraging behaviours where all stakeholders share their thoughts and opinions about the problem or issue. The essence of this style is about discussion and participation to identify common ground, share views and build and develop an acceptable outcome for all regarding the way ahead. However, like *Push* it has both advantages and disadvantages. The advantages are that it incorporates everybody's thoughts, ideas and views which can often lead to a richer solution; it gains commitment and can be developmental. The disadvantages are that it can appear wishy-washy or weak and it does take time, so it must be difficult to use in times of crisis or with deadline constraints.

When using *Pull* typical stages in the process are:

▶ Stating the situation and your view of it
▶ Testing how the other person sees the situation
▶ Exploring and discussing each others perspectives of the situation, working towards an agreement about the situation

▶ Working towards a solution taking account of each person's ideas and views – this is especially important if commitment is important.
▶ Reach a joint agreement as to the way ahead

As we said before – sticking to one style and using it all the time is probably a mistake. It is always best to consider the circumstances, the people and the problem and then select the appropriate approach in order to reach the most effective outcome. As rugby coach Nigel Melville suggests, no one style fits all situations; it's knowing when to use one or the other: 'You have to move up and down the continuum constantly, the real skill is judging when to use them, and in what quantity.'

COMMITMENT OR COMPLIANCE

Perhaps one of the most important things to consider is whether you require commitment or compliance to the issue/problem you are trying to influence. Commitment implies that others engage and work with you developing a sense of obligation and loyalty to supporting the influencer and their issue. Typically commitment requires a *Pull* style influencing approach – issues that require commitment are those which one must spend time over. Time must be invested in understanding the perspectives of all those involved and then working towards a solution and way ahead that everyone can buy into. Compliance implies conformity or obedience, and willingness for people to fall in line. This approach is appropriate if there is a safety, security or time issue at stake and the influencer has the position, power and authority to influence the decision and the way ahead. *Push* styles are often the most appropriate for this type of influencing situation.

While *Push* and *Pull* are the two basic styles or approaches, we have observed that within each of these styles there are two sub styles each of which uses slightly different techniques and skills and is appropriate under different circumstances. The styles are *Push* – Directive and persuasive reasoning and *Pull* – Collaborative and visionary.

We use this model to illustrate these styles:

We believe that most of us get 'stuck' using our preferred style and that by exploring different approaches and techniques you can develop the ability to vary your style to suit the situation and people and thus arrive at effective outcomes more elegantly.

THE FOUR STYLES

Each of the four styles has its own characteristics, upsides and downsides; no one style is a priori 'better' than another. Rather it is contextual, and thus important to select the right style (or combination of styles) for the people involved, the environment, the situation and the particular issue under discussion. Unfortunately most of us fall into the trap of overdependence on one style.

▶ **Directive** – this is an *'I' driven* style where people assert their own views and perspectives and expect others to follow. Typically people using this style will very clearly and specifically state their expectations, often using prescriptive dictatorial language. They will tend to come across as in command of themselves and others, demonstrating good knowledge in the topic area and a real belief in their ideas for the way ahead. They may tend to say things like 'I think we should do it …', or 'In my experience …' or 'There is only one way of dealing with this …'. The main aim appears to be to get people on board quickly in order to move ahead. People who are successful using this style are experts in their field with a high level of credibility; and they probably have a successful track record of introducing new ideas and managing major change initiatives. It should only be used by people who thoroughly know their topic and when the situation involves time constraints or where safety or security is at risk. It can also be successful if you are influencing people who are less knowledgeable or who lack self confidence in a situation. This approach will tend to fail dismally if used on or with people who are skilled and knowledgeable in the area being discussed or if you yourself have not established your own expertise and track record either with the people or in the type of situation you are influencing. In choosing to use this approach you must be aware that you are ignoring others' perspectives and that you may be seen as dogmatic and dictatorial. On the other hand certain people may find it appealing in that it clearly puts forward a course of action for others to follow, it is very straightforward and enables those involved to clearly understand their involvement and what's expected of them. Examples of when this approach might be successful include:

▷ When you the influencer are an expert in your field, and the project you are currently working on is under severe time constraint – you require others to act very quickly to get things done. Being directive about what, who and when can often be what's needed in this type of situation.

▷ When you are working with a group of relatively new or young and inexperienced people, they have little or no knowledge of the issue and situation themselves and require guidance and direction from someone more senior. The trick in this type of situation is to know when to use the directive approach and when to begin using others styles to develop their ability and use of initiative.

▷ When it is appropriate for the culture. For instance, Uzbekistan tends to have a structured and hierarchical culture or in certain organisational cultures where this style would be the norm.

▶ **Persuasive reasoning** – this is an *issue driven* style where the main aim is to get others to buy into your ideas. People who use this style are often regarded as analytical, logical and objective. People who are successful in using this style are always well prepared, having done their research and established the pro's and con's for their case. They will be action oriented and challenging in delivery. In debate they will be willing to take people on and to stick their neck above the parapet in terms of defending their argument and case. Sometimes their overly logical and rational approach can seem lacking in the emotional aspect of influencing and may cause them to be regarded as too aggressive or even arrogant by others. One of the major downsides of this approach is the belief that because they have spent time researching the issue their way is correct whereas they haven't done enough homework on other people's perspectives and views. This can lead to a lack of support or commitment from others to the issue.

People who are comfortable using this style tend to convey confidence in their voice and body language and are often articulate and eloquent in debate. Typical statements used by them are 'The fact is ...', 'Based on my research I think we should ...' or 'Let me state my views as to how we should deal with this ...'. This style works best when dealing with others of a similar level and who probably have knowledge and experience of the area under discussion and who feel comfortable and confident to enter into the debate and discussion. At a personal level it is probably also best when you have significant knowledge and experience in the area and added to this you strongly believe that your suggestions are correct. Failure to succeed using this style can relate to the approach in terms of how you convey your message to others, or your failure to back your case up with sufficient reasons and to convey to others your level of commitment to and belief in the issue. People do however, find this approach appealing and will often relate to it and buy in when you present a persuasive, articulate and convincing case for their support, especially if this is linked to a consistency of your behaviour in relation to the issue. Examples of when this approach is most successful include:

▷ When you have to gain buy in to an unpopular issue and you are the expert or are at least more knowledgeable than others in the area. You demonstrate that you have done your homework by presenting to all involved both sides of the case – advantages and disadvantages – and then you enable a debate around the issues.

▷ When you know there is a right and a wrong answer to an issue and you can demonstrate why by putting forward a rational well thought through case.

▷ When your expertise, track record and belief in an issue is well known to others and regarded highly by your stakeholders.

▶ **Collaborative** – this is a *team oriented* style where one of the main aims is to involve others in the whole process. Individuals who use this style will realise that they do not hold all the answers and they need input from others in order to reach an effective outcome. Success in using this style is all about consultation and collaboration with others. It will involve a whole variety of interpersonal skills – listening and building on others' ideas, questioning to gain a good understanding of each others' perspectives and use of appropriate paralanguage and body language during the process.

It will be important to demonstrate empathy, appreciation and patience. Gaining truly collaborative outcomes involves taking part in a process which demands patience and understanding. Typical statements a person using this style would use include, 'Let me check that I understand …', 'May I ask a question …', and 'Let's explore how that might work …'. This approach is most appropriate when you require long term buy in and involvement in making the issue a success. It is often particularly appropriate when dealing with change or issues where it is clear that there is no one correct answer. You may also believe the outcome would benefit from hearing from a broad range of people all of whom may have different views and perspectives about the issue. This approach may fail if you require a quick decision about an issue as the whole basis of the style is about discussion and involving others. It is also less likely to work with inexperienced people who are unaware of their environment, or lacking in knowledge about the situation. In addition you have to be aware of the potential downsides of this style which can be regarded as your not knowing your stuff as you have to involve so many others, or you could be seen as indecisive, or it could begin to involve too much information thus agreeing on a way ahead becoming very difficult. In our experience this style and approach is the most popular in today's business environment with many people using it to the exclusion of some of the others. It is important to recognise that while this style is highly involving and will, if used well, lead to collaborative outcomes that all the stakeholders can feel they have contributed to and thus bought into it is only one approach and as we have already implied it is best not to be overly reliant on one style but to develop the capability to use a range of styles during influencing discussions. Typical situations where this style is highly effective would be:

▷ Where you have just taken on responsibility for a project where your project management skills are necessary but you already know that you are not an authority on the topic. For instance, designing and implementing a new performance management system for a group of staff. You probably have a view on the subject but you know others will as well and in addition to this you are also aware that the whole issue is highly emotive. And, the bottom line is that you require commitment to the new process whatever it is.
▷ When creativity and new ideas are important.

▶ **Visioning** – a *people oriented* style where one of the main aims is to appeal to people's emotions in order to get them involved with your influencing issue. People who use this style are often deeply involved in their issue and demonstrate significant levels of personal value driven behaviour when influencing others. This approach demands that you are able to engage other's emotion and imagination, it appeals to people's feelings and is often appropriate when you wish to involve a lot of people at the same time. People who use this approach are typically highly articulate and confident public speakers who express themselves eloquently using appropriate vocal and body language. They are often inspirational or motivational people. Many famous orators have used and use this style to excite audiences – for instance, Bob Geldof when he launched Band Aid, Live Aid and Live 8, or Martin Luther King in Washington in August 1963.

On a less positive note this approach does not always have to be used in the common good and can be used to excite people about an issue in a very selfish way, for instance Hitler at the Nuremberg Rallies. Other downsides include the fact that it can appear lacking in detail or too abstract and vague and for some of us the level of enthusiasm and energy typically involved in using this style can be off putting. The sort of statements made by people who use this style include, 'Imagine …', 'Let me paint a picture of what might be if …', and 'What if …'. Using this style usually involves focussing on some point in the future and can involve creative approaches to presenting your ideas, for instance the use of metaphor, storytelling, pictures, diagrams and imagery. It is often used to kick start a project or change as a way of involving and exciting a wide range of people. It is not deemed to be very successful or appropriate when there are time constraints or set procedures or solutions. Frequently we experience people using this approach when,

▷ they want to engage people's interest and begin to whet their appetite to get them talking about an issue, for instance at the very beginning of a long-term and complex change.

▷ they want to encourage people to be creative and spend sometime thinking about a way ahead for an issue but at this point do not wish to get involved in detailed discussion.

I use Push/Sell/Cajole/Logic and Trust, but not always relying on any one particular method. But " trust me-I'm right," is a bit of a last resort. When we reach an impasse, I would usually say we will do this, if it fails it's my fault and we will review it.

Nigel Melville, Rugby Coach

The table that follows summarises and details for each approach the benefits, the problems, words that might be used to describe people using the approach, typical body and verbal language, words or phrases used, when its best to use and when best to avoid use.

| **Push** | | **Pull** | |
| Directive | *Persuasive* reasoning | Collaborative | Visionary |

Benefits

▶ Demonstrates good knowledge and belief in own case ▶ Gets straight to the point ▶ Is speedy ▶ Is clear in putting forward expectations ▶ Others know where they stand and what's expected	▶ Action oriented ▶ Ruthless in debate ▶ Appears to be well prepared and thought through ▶ Very clear in their thinking and action plan ▶ Often willing to challenge the status quo and take a risk	▶ Involves others in the whole process ▶ Gets buy in early on ▶ Demonstrates humility ▶ Shows respect for others ▶ Consultative in approach ▶ Usually involves building on others' ideas ▶ Can involve linking to others' ideas	▶ Engages others' emotions ▶ Can be infectious ▶ Appeals to people's feelings ▶ Can involve a lot of people at the same time ▶ Highly effective in times of change

Problems

▶ May appear a little dictatorial ▶ Can seem dogmatic ▶ Ignores others' perspectives ▶ not future orientated too focussed on the here and now ▶ Can lose support and loyalty ▶ Can be demotivational	▶ Could be seen as too assertive – even aggressive ▶ Could convey that their mind is already made up ▶ May choose the wrong battle ▶ Could win the battle but lose the war ▶ May have limited support and loyalty	▶ Takes a long time ▶ Could come across as not knowing their stuff ▶ Seen as indecisive ▶ Can't see wood for trees ▶ Could get too involved with too many perspectives ▶ Can appear wishy-washy	▶ Could appear to be Selfish ▶ Could come across as overly enthusiastic ▶ Can appear vague to some ▶ Too future oriented ▶ Can appear too abstract

Words to Describe This Approach

▶ Demanding ▶ Bargaining ▶ Prescriptive ▶ Authoritative ▶ Expert ▶ Judge ▶ Direct ▶ Command ▶ Order ▶ Tell ▶ Dictatorial ▶ Dogmatic	▶ Logical ▶ Factual ▶ Objective ▶ Rational ▶ Analytical ▶ Debating ▶ Consistent ▶ Reason ▶ Judicious ▶ Methodical	▶ Understanding ▶ Empathetic ▶ Involving ▶ Co-operative ▶ Compromising ▶ Common ground ▶ Inquisitive ▶ Trusting ▶ Thoughtful ▶ Supportive ▶ Appreciative	▶ Inspirational ▶ Energetic ▶ Articulate ▶ Passionate ▶ Expressive ▶ Aspirational ▶ Creative ▶ Innovative ▶ Motivational ▶ Eloquent ▶ Expressive ▶ Ingenious

Typical Body Language and Non-Verbal Communication

▶ Serious ▶ Hand gestures involving finger	▶ Focussed ▶ 'I' statements ▶ Assertive body language	▶ Matching others behaviour ▶ Relaxed	▶ Animated ▶ Excited ▶ Varied vocal tone

- pointing
- ▶ Confident, clear voice
- ▶ Domineering tone
- ▶ Strong eye contact
- ▶ Uses 'I'
- ▶ Rapport building
- ▶ Uses 'we'
- ▶ Uses images
- ▶ Uses stories and metaphors

Words or Phrases Which May be Used

- ▶ 'What I'll expect from you …'
- ▶ 'I'd like to tell you about …'
- ▶ Talks about the right way
- ▶ 'In my experience'
- ▶ 'I think we should do this …'
- ▶ 'I want to approach it this way …'
- ▶ 'The only way is …'

- ▶ 'Let me state my case'
- ▶ 'Recent research shows …'
- ▶ 'The fact is …'
- ▶ 'The way I see it is …'
- ▶ 'Based on my research I think we should …'

- ▶ 'Let me see if I understand …'
- ▶ 'Can I ask a question?'
- ▶ 'Here's a suggestion …'
- ▶ Talks about options and possibilities
- ▶ 'How would you approach this …'
- ▶ 'How do you think we could …'

- ▶ 'Imagine …'
- ▶ 'Let me paint you a picture of what could be.'
- ▶ 'I envisage …'
- ▶ 'Picture this …'
- ▶ 'what if …'

When to use

- ▶ When you know your subject thoroughly
- ▶ When you are regarded as an expert
- ▶ When you have high levels of credibility
- ▶ When time, security or safety are an issue
- ▶ When you clearly understand the issue and situation
- ▶ When you are working with less knowledgeable people

- ▶ When you are recognised as an expert with a track record of success
- ▶ When working with people of a similar level
- ▶ When you have done your homework
- ▶ When you believe strongly in something
- ▶ In certain situations

- ▶ When other people's long-term buy in and involvement is vital
- ▶ When you don't know all the answers
- ▶ When you need ideas from others
- ▶ When dealing with dilemmas or conundrums
- ▶ In times of uncertainty

- ▶ At the beginning of a major change programme
- ▶ To get people interested and talking
- ▶ To get things started
- ▶ To release people's creative thinking
- ▶ To gain enthusiasm
- ▶ For strategic issues

When to avoid using

- ▶ When you are not an expert
- ▶ When you have low or no established credibility
- ▶ When working with others who are experts

- ▶ When you can't back up your case with facts and research
- ▶ When you don't feel strongly about the issue

- ▶ When you need a quick decision
- ▶ When working with very inexperienced people

- ▶ In a hierarchical organisation or culture unless you are the boss.
- ▶ When surrounded by strong directives or persuasive reasoners
- ▶ When there are time constraints
- ▶ When there are set procedures
- ▶ When dealing with puzzles

It is our belief that no one style is more effective than any other and that the real skill in influencing involves developing the ability to diagnose the most appropriate style to use for the environment, situation and people and developing the skill to use all four styles. This means that during any influencing discussion you may find yourself using a range of styles – often we find that people start with a visionary approach where they set out their big picture ideas and whet people's appetite to want to talk more. Then they move to persuasive reasoning where they set out their particular view of the situation but possibly also recognise that they need the support of others and thus move on to the collaborative in order to explore and work with others to gain commitment to action. Sometimes people finish off with the directive approach as it can be useful to help identify what you believe to be the major benefit and the costs if nothing is done.

On many occasions we have experienced people using this approach and one particular case study that comes to mind involves two colleagues using the range of styles while doing a double act presentation.

CASE STUDY

The whole management team had been called together by the managing director and his deputy to attend a meeting about the future of the organisation. There was a real buzz in the room as most people were aware of the possible sale of the organisation, but were also aware that a management buy out had been on the cards. The two gentleman in question – let's call them Jim and Bob – took to the stage. Jim who was the MD opened the proceedings with an extremely visionary presentation about the organisation, how it had got to where it was today and his ideas for the future, then he handed over to Bob his deputy. Bob continued the process in a far more structured way using the persuasive reasoning approach where he laid out the current state of affairs and presented the ideas for the future of the organisation which involved the organisation being merged (or was it a buy out!)with another well known player in the industry – he presented both the pros and cons in an extremely rational and factual manner – clearly he'd done his homework. Before he handed back to Jim to finish off he moved into directive mode when he briefly indicated the severe risks associated with not buying into what they were suggesting. To finish off Jim returned to the spotlight and made an impassioned plea which indicated that the organisation had got to where it was today by involving all the management and staff and he believed that if the merger was to be a success this collaborative approach was necessary to move ahead. So he was going to set up a process to take place over the following seven days where he and Bob together with other senior team members would facilitate group discussions to hear as many people's points of view as was possible before the final decision was made.

Ten days later the announcement was made that the organisation was 'merging' with one of its competitors and that it had the backing and commitment of the majority of its staff and management. Jim and Bob had pulled it off and to this day I believe that the process they adopted in telling their colleagues was instrumental in the success of the whole takeover.

Another way of looking at the styles might be to create certain character profiles – you may recognize some of the following types:

The tough guy uses the persuasive reasoning style as their main influencing approach. They will be fluent in debate, happy to put forward their point of view and to defend it with a well thought through case. They come across as so confident and well prepared, that they are often difficult to challenge or even engage in discussion with. They will be action oriented; if they are successful they will have a good track record of effective influencing and high levels of credibility in their organisation. Used ineffectively it is seen as bullying and competitive, and will eventually turn people off.

The best friend uses predominantly collaborative approaches, possibly with some emotion thrown in. They want to involve all the other stakeholders in discussion. They will tend to indicate that they do not have all the knowledge or answers but want to reach a consensus view before moving to action. They truly believe that getting buy in throughout the influencing process is vital for long-term success. Often they are regarded by the tough guy types as weak and wishy-washy, and can be bulldozed by this type. Highly rational people may also find this approach tiresome. The biggest downside of this type is the time involved in the whole process. However, if we are to accept that influencing is 'a process and not an event' then this type of approach is vital for all to be comfortable with.

The bull in the china shop uses the directive style and takes up challenges and is driven by their own emotional response to situations. They conclude something is wrong or someone has been unfairly treated – and off they go. Over reliance on emotion, and lack of rationality and of reflection are their biggest disadvantages. On the other hand, this style can be very appealing if you are in agreement about the issue and simply want someone to tell you what to do in the situation.

The idealist relies heavily upon the visionary approach usually because of their unswerving belief in the issue they are attempting to influence you about. Often carried away with their own commitment to an issue or idea they can be blinded by their own faith. On the other hand and on a more positive note the idealist can convey enthusiasm and total belief through their own emotional involvement in a topic often encouraging people to go along with them because of this belief.

THE INFLUENCING CONTINUUM

In addition to the above variety of styles, there is also a continuum about the level of importance people attach to influencing and the need for it.

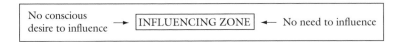

Despite the changes we outlined in the introduction, there are still people in organisations who have never developed the belief that influencing is necessary – especially people who through their working life have managed to get by using power and position. This has never been a winning strategy long-term: as A.J.P. Taylor said of Lord Northcliffe '*He aspired to power instead of influence and as a result forfeited both.*' Some might also say that Margaret Thatcher in the latter part of her premiership demonstrated no real desire to use influence and was overly dependent on position and power (in fact she is quoted as saying '*consensus is the negation of leadership*'). People like this reside at the left-hand side of the spectrum.

At the right-hand end of our spectrum are those lucky people who throughout their life have had no need to influence. There are three main groups here – people who have the luxury of choosing their work mates, people who work alone, and people who are just plain lucky!

The rest of us reside in 'the influencing zone' and need to select the most effective skills, approach, style and strategies to ensure successful outcomes.

Understanding your own preference regarding style can be particularly useful not only to help you identify your own particular strengths and development areas but also as a means of introducing you to other styles and approaches which you may find useful when influencing others.

Exercise

Examine the four scenarios below and reflect upon the most appropriate influencing style or styles to adopt in getting others to work with you to achieve your goal.

Scenario	Style/s
1. You are put in charge of a project to introduce a new performance appraisal system to your organisation. You have been with the organisation for several years and have a reputation of 'getting things done'. Your first challenge is to enlist the help of others to join the project team and then to encourage others to offer their ideas and thoughts for incorporation into the project outcome.	
2. You are one of four departmental managers who are working together to create a new brochure advertising your company's full product range. Until recently the brochure has been the responsibility of one of this group. Owing to a change of CEO it has been decided to revamp the company's image and one important way of doing this it to update the brochure. You have for some time thought that the old approach was a bit outdated, however, you do not wish to upset your colleague by telling him so. You do however wish to make sure your ideas are heard and considered by the group.	
3. You are regarded as your company's expert on public relations and your boss has asked you to raise the company's profile in the local area. You have to influence your management team colleagues to take part in a photo shoot for the local paper but some of them are being a bit bashful.	
4. You are planning a charity event to raise money for the local hospice and wish to get ideas from your colleagues about the form it should take, the aim being to encourage as many people as possible to attend.	

Suggested Answers

1. In this situation probably the best approach is to use a *Pull* style starting with a visionary style and then possibly moving to a collaborative style. The aim in this circumstance is to first get people's interest and then to encourage them to work with you to share ideas and thoughts.
2. Clearly in this situation you feel strongly about the subject, wish to get your point across and the people involved are all your peers. Under these circumstances a persuasive reasoning approach is probably the most fitting. When the people involved are at the same level as you,

have their own views and feel open and capable of sharing them with you then stating your case plainly and openly is appropriate.

3. As an expert and assuming you have some degree of credibility within the organisation you have earned yourself the right to use the directive approach.

4. In this situation the collaborative approach is the most apposite. When those you are attempting to influence have no need to follow you it is important to get the influencee's voluntary commitment.

IDENTIFYING AND DEVELOPING YOUR STYLE

Understanding and recognising your own preferred influencing style can be particularly helpful to your overall skill as an influencer. Knowing your preference will help you to understand where you might focus your development to be more effective in a broader range of situations. We believe that developing your capability to use a range of different styles to suit the people, issue and situation will help you enormously when influencing others.

✍ SUMMARY OF KEY POINTS

- ☞ People tend to develop a preference in terms of the style they depend upon when influencing others.
- ☞ Over reliance on one style can have its disadvantages and we believe that developing the capability to use a range of styles is beneficial for influencing success.
- ☞ Understanding whether you require *compliance or commitment* will help you to determine the most appropriate style.
- ☞ There are two basic approaches – *Push and Pull.*
  - ☞ *Push* is a tell approach which is more appropriate when compliance is required.
  - ☞ *Pull* is a sell approach which is more appropriate when commitment is needed.
- ☞ There are two *Push styles – directive and persuasive reasoning.*
- ☞ There are two *Pull styles – collaborative and visionary.*
- ☞ Determining which style is your preference and which styles you avoid can help you to identify where you need to develop in order to become a more effective influencer.

5 Awareness of Others
'Standing in Their Shoes'

> *Understanding the triggers in others and what underlying motives they have is key.*
>
> Participant – Ashridge Influencing Strategies
> and Skills Programme

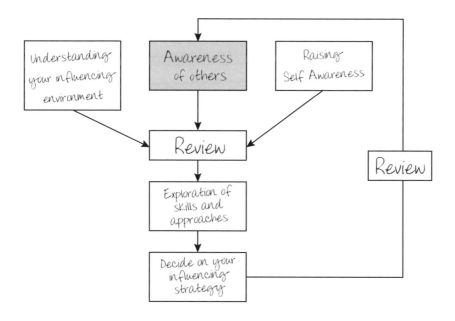

A MODEL FOR INFLUENCING

One of the key elements of the Model is awareness of others. We find in our seminars and consulting work, that many managers can have a fairly large blind spot here. They just do not seem to be that interested in reading others and adapting their style to the other person. They have an approach and they stick to it, irrespective of how effective that approach actually is.

Planning and preparing

People often feel that to be a successful influencer is to be like a successful speaker – to have charisma, confidence and fluidity. To be able to make off the cuff remarks, to be verbally fluent and to have a way with words are considered to be the key skills. Clearly it can be useful to possess these talents, but we find that what characterises the most effective influencers is their attention to preparation. As the nineteenth-century American writer and author of Tom Sawyer and Huckleberry Finn Mark Twain said – 'It usually takes me more than three weeks to prepare a good impromptu speech.'

When we need to influence others our first task is to try and understand them.

► Who are they?
► What are their hopes, their fears?
► What context are they operating in?
► What are their concerns?
► What turns them on?
► What turns them off?

If you don't know the answer to most of these questions, you are unlikely to be as effective an influencer as you could be!

If you can, you need to do some research. That could involve interviewing people from the organisation or their clients. If you don't have time, it might just be a case of looking up the organisation on the internet. Or you could ask your network if anyone knows that particular organisation (something we do regularly at Ashridge). An excellent example of someone planning and preparing in advance in order to win over an audience occurred back in the late 1970s when I went to see the American rock band The Eagles play a concert in Scotland. Many rock stars limit their preparation (apart from the music rehearsals of course) to learning a word or two of the language of a particular country (of the 'Bonjour Paris' type).

In this case the lead guitarist Joe Walsh came on stage, said hello Scotland and we all groaned. But this time it was different. He wanted to introduce us to a friend he said, and on strolled a Scottish Pipe Major, resplendent in full regalia of kilt, bearskin hat and sporran. Not bad, we thought, he has gone to the trouble of finding out some of our traditions and inviting someone to come and play bagpipes for a song. Up they went in our esteem. That would have been impressive enough but what he did next really influenced the audience. A roadie brought on a set of bagpipes and Walsh proceeded to play a duet with the Piper on the bag-pipes! Bagpipes are notoriously difficult to play – in fact in Scotland peo-ple learning to play them are often seen strolling around in a park or other spot far removed from houses as the noise made by beginners is appalling. Here was a busy guy, on a hectic schedule of European tour, who had taken the trouble to learn to play our national instrument. We are not suggesting that everyone can go to such lengths but the principle is the same. What can you learn about the people you want to influence?

If you cannot learn anything about them, then you are condemned to either guess, or worse, just do the same as you have always done. There is an expression in Neuro Linguistic Programming – 'If you always do what you always did, you will always get what you always got!'

So there are basically two rules here:

▶ find out where others are coming from, what matters to them.
▶ adapt what you have to say so that it makes sense to *them*.

There are a number of tools and techniques we can use to help our preparation. We find Influencing Network and Stakeholder mapping to be particularly useful.

MY INFLUENCING STAKEHOLDER NETWORK

Take a clean sheet of paper and in the middle write your name. Put a circle round it, then draw some lines radiating out of the circle. Now start to write in the names of the people you have to influence on a regular basis. You will probably need to write down the names of your spouse or partner, kids if you have them, parents, brothers and sisters. Friends will appear too.

You will find your boss's name is there, along with your colleagues and direct reports. Perhaps your boss's boss too. The names of people you have to interact with in other companies may appear and if you have clients they will appear too. Key people in other departments of your organisation will also be there. In our case we will add our participants to the Network. Maybe you will add the people you work with in project groups, joint ventures, research committees, ad hoc teams and so on.

You may well be surprised by the number of people you influence reg-ularly. But *how* do you influence these people? In the same way? It's hardly likely that they all have the same personalities, concerns and preferences.

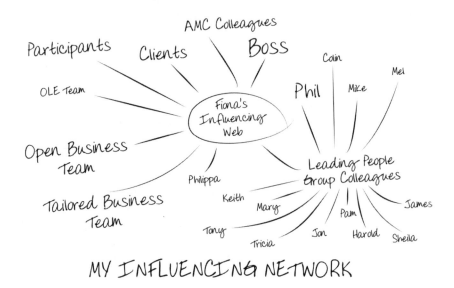

MY INFLUENCING NETWORK

In reality this example will be much more complex, crowded and detailed, however it should give you a rough idea of what it will look like. The main reason for doing this exercise is to illustrate just how complex your range of influencing relationships can be. In addition to this, the network drawing can be extremely helpful when working on specific issues.

It can help you to identify the people you need to influence, and if you keep your network drawing reasonably up to date, it can act as a memory jogger to ensure you don't forget about a key stakeholder. This is easy to do and can have significant consequences for your effectiveness and success.

STAKEHOLDER MAPPING

Another tool we use for preparation is the stakeholder map. This is an attempt to actually map out the key stakeholders in any specific Influencing Issue.

Again we take a clean sheet of paper – preferably A3 size. This time we write the issue in the centre and start to draw in the key stakeholders for this particular issue. In our example (see the figure titled A stake holder map) we use the redesign of a development programme at Ashridge to illustrate.

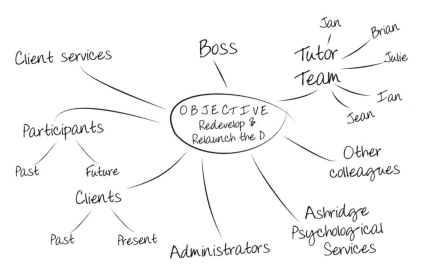

A STAKEHOLDER MAP

Once we have drawn in the stakeholders the next task is to ask ourselves some questions about each of these people. How important are they to the issue – can you prioritise them?

▶ What power do they hold? (see later for a more detailed discussion on power)
▶ What's in it for them?
▶ What is your relationship with them like? Is it positive or negative or just somewhere in the middle?

Peter Block (1987) says that those whom we need to influence become our adversaries or allies based on two dimensions – agreement and trust.

▶ So how much trust is there? To be specific, how much do you trust them? How much do they trust you?
▶ To what extent do they agree or disagree with you on the issue?
▶ How much do they share your perspective on an issue? A lot? A little? Not at all?
▶ If the answer is not at all, what *is* their perspective?
▶ What are their hopes? What do they want to get out of the situation?
▶ What are their fears?

▶ What language do they typically use? Do they talk about pushing things through or gaining support? Do they talk about logic or feelings? Do they talk about winners and losers or about participants?

▶ Do they have a preference in terms of how they like information to be presented to them?

EXAMPLE

Roy Jenkins (2001) tells us in Winston Churchill's biography that Churchill had a clear preference for written information and was famously poor at listening to others' points of views. However if someone had an opinion and took the trouble to write to him, he was able to read it and take their position seriously. His wife Clementine advised Churchill's friend General Spears to 'Put what you have to say in writing. He (Churchill) often does not listen or does not hear if he is thinking of someone else. But he will always consider a paper seriously and take in all its implications. He never forgets what he sees in writing.'

The next stage in the process is to annotate the Map with the detail about each person. These notes then serve as a planning document which can help you decide upon the process you will adopt in terms of your styles, skills and strategies.

STAKEHOLDER MAP - THE DETAIL

POWER AND INFLUENCE

Power and influence are inextricably linked – many books are written about influencing without authority, but when we influence we are usually using some type of power. There is quite a debate about what is actually meant by the word power, or how to define or measure it. For example one of the leading writers on the subject, Steven Lukes believes that consensual authority, where there is no conflict of interests, is not a form of power. Consensual authority is where a person has voluntarily entered into a contract or understanding with another party. So, for example, if my boss tells me to do something, and I obey, then he or she is not actually using power, but consensual authority, in the sense that I have joined the company of my own free will, and that I accept that some form of authority might be necessary to get the job done.

However most of us use the word power on a daily basis in everyday life, and we really don't think about defining it. We just moan that we don't have enough of it, that those in our organisation who do have it are somehow responsible for the problems we encounter. We think about how we can get more power, how power should be used, how to limit the power of those who have it. But we tend to think that others have more power than we do, and we often overestimate the extent and usefulness of that power, while underestimating our own sources of power.

We believe that in daily life we subtly use different types of power to influence or to boost our influence. It is perfectly acceptable to influence other people, even when there are disagreements about goals and objectives. On the other hand, where there is true conflict of interest, Lukes says we are not talking about influence but about power. So if I want to influence someone to do something that is against their own best interests – let's say making someone redundant – then I will not be using influence but a form of power. But does it matter?

The fact is that even if I have consensual authority there is very little agreement about what that consensus is. Sometimes I obey my boss because I agree with her, sometimes I disagree but obey anyway, because it doesn't really bother me. However, if I disagree with her fundamentally, I might pretend to obey her by saying yes, and then not do whatever it was, or, do it badly, so that I wouldn't get asked again.

The relationship between influence and power is therefore an uneasy and unclear one.

In this book, although we focus on influencing when there is no direct power, we feel it is important to examine the different types of power available. Many managers consider that position or hierarchical power would be enough to obtain compliance, and that they would therefore not need to be able to influence. Keith Grint, lecturer at Lancaster University Business School, pointed out in his book *Fuzzy Management* (1997) that power should be considered as a relationship because it can only be delivered *through* a relationship and also because the execution of power is dependent, not on the manager's demand, for example, but through the employees' actions. Power relationships are therefore, we believe, relationships of influence. If they were not, it would be enough for a manager to get compliance by simply saying 'Do this!' and the employee would do it, rather like parents just saying to their children, 'go to bed at once!' and the children rushing off immediately to bed without another word! Hardly likely is it?

If it is difficult to get kids to obey you, it is even more unlikely that a mature adult would simply obey another adult just because he/she is notionally in charge. So even if you have some position power in your organisation it is not going to be enough to make you a great influencer. You need to think about the nature and quality of your relationships, the skills and strategies you have, and the personal conviction, enthusiasm and arguments you bring to the situation.

The most obvious power in organisations is hierarchical or position power. This is also known as 'sacking' power, because the person who wields it is the person who has the power to fire us. There are several important things we need to know about power when we want to influence effectively. One is that there are different types of power – hierarchical power is not the only one. Etzioni (1973) wrote about two main types – Position or Formal power and Persona/Personal power.

Other researchers have classified power into five, six or seven categories depending on who you read. For example under *formal power* we find:

Reward power   Here those who are able to give desired rewards have a source of power. There are, of course, different types of rewards, ranging from material rewards like an increase in salary or position to social rewards such as recognition, praise etc. We tend to think of the people with reward power as being fairly high up the hierarchy, but that would be a mistake. Clearly they may have more control over resources and thus are able to potentially offer more material rewards. However, we all have a degree of reward power, and it is important to think carefully about what rewards we can give, and how others want to be rewarded by us. People may want recognition and thanks more than anything else. They may want to feel involved in a project or have their opinions taken seriously. Think of the people you work with and need to influence regularly. Do you know what type of rewards they value? And don't just think of monetary rewards! One of our colleagues regularly tells me that the most effective thing his boss could do to influence him is not to give him a pay rise, but to recognise his efforts and thank him for them.

We can include *Resource power* in here too. If you have access to, or control of scarce and desired resources then you have an effective source of power. Again, you may feel that you don't have much power, but reflect on what resources you have access to that perhaps more senior people do not. American academic and researcher Jeffrey Pfeffer tells us that among the most important resources you can have are allies and supporters. The flatter the organisation the more important it is to have allies and to have a good network. You are just as likely to develop networks through effective communication and rapport building skills, as through any formal position in the organisation. Take a moment to think of the size and quality of your own networks. Do you have a network that you can call on? Do you go out of your way to grow this network? Do you regularly keep in touch with those in your network, both inside and outside the organisation? Managers frequently tell us that they are too busy to do this. But in the light of the above finding, can you afford *not* to have a good network of contacts, allies and supporters?

Author and consultant Peter Block writes that the power of position is overrated. He tells us that even those at the top are actually in the middle. This is borne out by our conversations with hundreds of senior managers. There is always someone with more clout than you! The result is that the ability to influence becomes more important than your hierarchical position. The problem is that it often seems easier to use your position, which results in compliance at best, rather than engaging in the influencing process to gain commitment.

Coercive power   If you can punish people or physically force them to do something then you have coercive power. This can range from executing and imprisoning people through to punishing your kids by withholding pocket money or not allowing them to do something they want to do. Hopefully there is not too much coercion in your organisation, but in reality there is a fair amount of subtle coercive power being used in organisations. Hopefully there is no physical coercive power being used, but there may be the threat of punishment if you do not obey someone or carry out their instructions. There is a link to reward power in that the person who can punish can usually reward as well. As a parent for example you can influence by either rewarding good behaviour with extra pocket money, gifts and other desired rewards, or punish by withholding pocket money, grounding the kids, refusing to let them attend a concert etc.

In this book we are more interested in how you can influence without using coercive power. Coercion can backfire, it is a very blunt instrument with lots of pitfalls, and does very little to create commitment. Long-term commitment will not be achieved through coercion.

Legitimate power   Here the power resides in the position. The person using it has a legitimate right to ask you to do something, a Police officer, for example, or your boss. Once off duty or outside the office the officer or your boss has no right to use this power. In general, legitimate power has less weight than it used to – certainly in Europe and the US. This then implies that managers will have to rely less and less on their formal, legitimate power and more on other types of power and influence.

Information power   Here it is a case of what you know. It is not just managers who have inside information though. Many employees will have more information about a process or a client than the boss. We know from research that employees value managers who share information with them. Often companies keep a lot of information hidden. Informally many managers we have met talk about the Mushroom management style of their organisations, that is keep employees in the dark and cover them with manure!

So, in an influencing situation, reflect on what you know – about the subject, the people involved, the process etc. You can leverage this information, either by sharing the information and thus helping your colleagues or manager, for example, or by applying this knowledge to the influencing situation. To take a simple example: imagine you are buying a car from someone. You need the car urgently, but you will keep this information from the seller, because if they know the urgency they can use that information to stick to the price they are asking. If they discover the urgency then they will have the upper hand in the influencing process. But what if you also have some information concerning the seller? What if they are in desperate need of the money? Perhaps they have some financial difficulties and their bank is demanding funds immediately? If this is the case then they will want to keep this a secret from you. However if you have found this information then you are in a much better position to influence the price.

We have already suggested that planning and preparing are a key aspect of Influencing, so find out as much as you can about a situation before you attempt to influence.

And under *personal power* we find:

Expert power   This is one of the key power bases in today's organisations. We call on experts in all areas of life and it is an excellent way to influence others. Clearly, your credibility as an expert must be established if you are to influence others. But in general, we like experts and are quite trusting of them. We have a tendency to put our faith in them and believe experts in many areas, for instance, medical doctors, lawyers, engineers, etc. However perhaps there is a growing tendency to question experts these days – we are certainly less afraid to seek out second or third opinions.

If you are proposing a course of action and are seen as credible and competent in an area, then your influencing ability increases. You need therefore to establish your expertise, by being credible and trustworthy. So how do you establish your credibility? It can be by doing a good job, by being referred by others who are trusted. It may be that your credentials are good – you have excellent qualifications for example and you have worked with reputable organisations and other well known and respected people. The key thing though is that you must convince others of your expertise. You can not take it for granted.

You need to demonstrate in some way your expertise, and you need to be confident. This area of power is perhaps the one which you can use the most to influence others. We, for example would consider ourselves as having high expertise in the field of executive education. But how do we show that expertise to out clients?

In one sense we are lucky because Ashridge already had an excellent reputation. It has existed as a management college for some forty-five years and as a building goes all the way back to the thirteenth century! We are accredited by the major accreditation authorities, and have high rankings in the various league tables proposed in the media such as the *Financial Times* and *Newsweek*. When participants come here they can see that this is no fly by night type of place. The building, the resources, the number of managers from respected companies and organisations from many different countries, all speak of durability and competence.

If we had to teach a seminar in a motorway hotel, for example, we would have to work a lot harder to establish our credibility. When we work in China for example, where Ashridge is not particularly well known, we will perhaps show some pictures of the college, tell our participants what kind of blue chip companies we have worked with all over the globe, and show extracts from the league tables – in order to establish that credibility. We have, for example, two business cards – one with just a name on it which we might use in Europe and North America, and one with a title and list of qualifications, which we might use in Asia.

We might hand out, or send in advance, some of the articles or books we have written. But what we are definitely aware of is the need to establish credibility and confidence, and thus our expertise – and not take it for granted

So how do *you* establish *your* expertise?

▶ Do you just assume that everyone will know you have expertise?
▶ Do you speak with authority on your subject or are you hesitant?

▶ Have you considered writing articles?

▶ Have you spoken on your area to students or to other experts?

▶ How much do you read?

▶ How much do you keep up to date with what is happening in your field?

▶ How do you dress? If you are a research scientist, used to dressing fairly casually and informally, do you change to a suit and tie when making a proposal to your senior managers?

▶ Do you speak their language (chance of success, feasibility, profitability, cost etc.) or your language (research, interesting, possibility)?

> Knowledge in my field is my strength. I am the expert and accepted as such. When the oracle speaks then everyone agrees.

Participant, Ashridge
Influencing Strategies and Skills Programme, 2004

Referent power   is the type of power which is linked to the group or people we identify with. This includes peer pressure, endorsements etc. For example nine year old Louis is a keen footballer and staunch Manchester United fan. He has never seen them play but watches them on television, buys magazines and posters, keeps up to date with who they play, where they play, who is in the team and out, who is injured, who is playing well. He has Manchester United football strips, and boots. He refers to Manchester United and is strongly influenced by anything to do with them. If there were Manchester United baked beans he would probably try to convince his mum to buy that brand. His other referent group will be his peers at school – so if a certain type of training shoe is in vogue with them, he will hassle his Mum to buy that brand and not another one.

Thirteen year old Joel wants to upgrade his phone. He has exactly the same model as we have. We travel all over the world, (so the tri-band facility is essential) use the mobile on a daily basis for business as well as personal calls. The specs are more than adequate for this fairly intensive use.

But Joel isn't satisfied. He doesn't travel around the world, only uses it for texts and mostly local calls to his pals. When asked why he needs a better phone than us, what does he respond? Not that he is about to become a consultant and start visiting China, Japan and the US. No, his friends all have the latest model, so he wants one as well. This is incredibly influential – here is a 13 year old who is prepared to spend more than £10 a month getting a contract with a telephone company simply to get the latest in vogue phone model.

Advertisers are keenly aware of this and one of the most popular advertising techniques is to have stars endorse products or services. The influence is stronger when a star endorses a product they obviously use – like a golfer using a certain type of club or tennis star using a particular racket. Where it gets murky is when that same star starts advertising drinks, clothes and washing up products – then their credibility is lessened.

How does this affect influencing at work?

If I want to persuade a group of people that a new book on leadership for example, or a new psychometric questionnaire is useful, I first need to think of who their referent group is. As academics and trainers it is likely to be other respected academics trainers and perhaps researchers. So I will look firstly for one respected and neutral person to endorse the product. This will influence some members of the group to try the product. Another referent group for trainers are course participants. So if I carry out the questionnaire on a participant (let's say from a well known company who is already a good client) at no cost, and get their endorsement, then this will also bring referent power into play for the group I want to influence. If I want to be clever about this I will also have chosen someone who has referent power himself within the organisation so they can influence others – like the training department in their organisation (thus indirectly bringing in more referent power to bear on my colleagues).

Another aspect to referent power is charisma – how you are liked and valued by others. We have seen many teams in companies where the person with the formal, position power does not actually wield the real power. The group looks first of all to the person who is looked up to in the group, the person whose personality they admire. In football for example there are many teams where the captain is less respected than someone who has no official position, but has the respect of the other players.

There is an ongoing debate about charisma – what it is exactly, and are you born with it or can you learn it. What is clear to us is that you can learn to have more impact on others, by being empathetic, building rapport, being interested in others, listening more, and by working on your voice, body language and dress.

Understanding your power

An important thing to understand is your own power and the power of the person or group of people you are influencing. Typically people in organisations overestimate or underestimate their power. Often managers will overestimate their hierarchical power. Many imagine that because they have a strong hierarchical position people will automatically obey them or that they will wield strong influence without having to do anything else.

On the other hand, those being managed typically underestimate their own power; they see that they do not have the boss's hierarchical power and that they have no other power at their disposal.

If we look at an example within our organisation we can illustrate how this works. One of our colleagues, a trainer and consultant, does not have a lot of formal hierarchical power, and of course he has less than his boss. So influencing his boss by trying to use hierarchical power simply isn't on. So what kind of power does he have? Well, he has a considerable amount of expert power in the sense that he can teach group dynamics, team building, leadership, strategy, coaching and other subjects. He is fluent in Dutch and German, has written a number of articles and books, has gained two Doctorate degrees, and has specific experience of various techniques and cultures. He has network power in the sense that he has contacts and networks of clients, colleagues and participants that no one else has. He also has friends and contacts among people in South Africa who have changed that country's culture and direction – giving him a lot of credibility when talking about Leadership for example.

So it is important for you to know what power and how much power you bring into an influencing situation. Clearly, I cannot influence my CEO using hierarchical power, but rather than not trying to influence, I might try to use expert power or network/relationship power if I have them in that particular scenario. In order to be an effective influencer I need to look at each influencing issue and decide just what power I have in that situation. I then try to leverage that power in the situation.

If I do not have any network or expert power in a situation I would need to fall back on argument or use my persuasion or influencing power. Managers are telling us that they cannot rely on position power any more. Either they have it and people simply do not respond to it (there is low unemployment in this country, and people with skills are in high demand), or they quite simply do not have strong positional power any more – they have what is called 'Dotted line' responsibility. They could work in a matrix organisation or in project groups or ad hoc teams where there are no clear reporting and position power. So if they cannot use position power what can they do? Clearly they can exploit other types of power if they have them, or they will need to improve their influencing skills using the kinds of tools and techniques we outline in this book.

EXAMPLE

One excellent use of power in influencing happened when I was travelling back to the UK with a colleague from an assignment in Germany. We were about to board our flight when there was an announcement in German – my German is pretty rusty and I struggled to understand what it was, but I feared it was to announce a delay in the flight. I did catch something about four hours, and prayed that this was not to be an announcement of a four hour delay! I looked around and everything was calm – none of the usual disgruntled complaints and agitation that would normally follow such an announcement on a Friday evening! So I thought it was just my poor grasp of the language and that there was nothing to worry about!

Then the announcer switched to English and sure enough my fears were confirmed – there was to be a four hour delay! But even now there was no agitation, no anger – everything stayed very calm. Why? Because suddenly people had decided to take a Zen approach to delays? Not at all – the Lufthansa staff had done something very clever … . Realising the effect of a four hour delay on passengers at 6 pm on a Friday evening, they had asked the Captain himself to come and make the announcement. The sight and sound of the Captain making the announcement, plus his skill at doing it – very apologetic but also very clear that it was beyond his and the airline's control – ensured that the passengers remained very calm. Of course the Captain receives much more respect than an ordinary member of staff does – they have more gravitas and authority, and no one questioned his announcement. They also did something else rather well that evening … they managed expectations. Often an airline announces a one hour delay only for that to turn in to a two or three hour delay. In this case the Captain had announced the worst case scenario, but told us that he and his crew would be ready to fly if there was a change in Air Traffic Control. So off we went in search of a coffee, prepared for a four hour delay. One hour later Lufthansa announced that they were ready and we could board the flight. So all in all we suffered a 75 minute delay in total silence and absolute calm – in fact feeling quite positive about the whole thing!

Exercise

You may find it useful to reflect about this whole area of power by considering some of the following questions:

► In general what are your power bases in your job?
► What power bases can you draw upon in your personal life?

▶ Can any of the ones you have in your personal life help in your job, and vice versa?

▶ Think of some recent influencing issues you have dealt with and reflect on the power bases you had in relation to them. Did you use them or not? If so, how and what was the outcome?

POWER TACTICS

How do we translate our power bases into actions? Assuming that you can identify your various power bases, it is important to consider how you can best use them. Different tactics are available and studies (Ansari *et al.*, 1990; Kipnis *et al.*, 1980) show that the most common tactics are:

Reason – using facts, logic etc. to back up one's point of view.

Assertiveness – being directive, making commands etc., demanding compliance.

Bargaining – proposing an exchange (For example, if you do X then I will do Y).

Friendliness – creating goodwill, being nice and friendly, asking politely.

Coalition – getting others involved, getting support from peers and others.

Higher authority or 'The Boss wants it done'. – As its' name implies this means getting someone with position power to back you up.

Sanctions – making threats, making promises, for example promising a salary increase or threatening to withhold a desired promotion.

The main tactic used in companies was the use of reason. Whether it was managers influencing subordinates or managers attempting to influence upwards, the use of reason dominated.

This is consistent with our own findings at Ashridge. Use of sanctions is usually a last resort approach, but it is important to be able to use all the strategies, to be skilled and flexible, and not just be stuck using one. For example, in cross cultural situations, you might have to move from your preferred strategy to one which you are not so used to. We know that in the USA managers tend to use reason as a preferred influencing strategy. In China however, managers tend to use coalition and higher authority. This is because the culture favours the indirect approach and there is a strong hierarchical power framework. Having worked several times in China my personal experience backs this up. Participants there have difficulty in using different types of influencing approaches because so much is done using *guanxi* – the indirect, relational approach, or through simple hierarchical and positional power.

A manager will choose an approach depending on one or more of several variables:

▶ The manager's relative power
▶ The manager's objectives for influencing
▶ The manager's expectation of the person's compliance
▶ The organisational culture
▶ Cross cultural differences

Look at the variables mentioned above. You will need to take these into consideration each time you decide on an influencing strategy, for example, we would be less likely to use hierarchical or positional power in a country like Sweden than in Uzbekistan.

If my relative power in a situation is low, then I am likely to use bargaining and friendliness, for example, rather than assertiveness or the threat of sanctions.

Power is also gained through relationships. Networking, staying close to people, knowing what is going on in the company and who is doing what can be very useful. If you do not network, if you think that politics is beneath you, then you are likely to have a lower influencing profile. Robert Reich tells us that to exercise influence in the White House when Bill Clinton was the U.S. President, you had to be close to him, be around when an issue came up, or have an office close to him. To be influential you had to be there!

NEGATIVE POWER

An example of the importance of negative power is given in the *Guardian* (16 June 2005). When rock star Bono was lobbying the US administration to help support his anti poverty campaign, he met Les Gelb from US think tank – the Council for Foreign Relations. Gelb did not give Bono the names of people who could help him, but the names of the people who could block him. Bono and his team then took these people on one by one.

The implications are that you will need to think about who has negative power in relation to any project or issue you are working on. Who might stop you? Who might block you? For what reasons? As in Bono's example it is likely that the best strategy will be to tackle these people individually and not in a group! Try to win them over one at a time.

To sum up, we need to be aware of our own sources of power, and those of the people around us. Not only in order to become effective influencers, but as Stephen Lukes (2005) writes 'If we are to have a chance of surviving and flourishing'. (p. 65)

SEARCHING FOR MUTUAL PERSPECTIVE

Often we frame a perspective for ourselves and not others – we look at the situation from our own particular standpoint and forget, or are unable to look at it from any other perspective. If we do not frame for common things then we are less likely to be effective in our influencing.

So how do we accomplish this? The first thing is that we have to explore our own position. Why do we hold this position? Is it a dogmatic position or is it a viable and pragmatic position? If it is the for-mer- can we reconsider our position in order to make it a more viable position vis a vis the people we want to influence? If it is the latter – we still need to think about how other people view our position The second thing therefore is that we have to explore the other person's perspective.

How do they see our position? Does it seem unreasonable? Do they think we are just being selfish. Are they thinking that we have fully considered their perspective or just our own? We need to ask, probe and discover the other person's positions and perspectives.

Once we have a good idea of their issues and concerns we can start to frame our position in such a way that it takes into account their positions (see section on reframing in chapter 6). For example, if I want to take a sabbatical from my work for four months in order to read, research and write more, then I have a number of ways in which I can influence my boss. I can take my usual approach of saying I am fed up, haven't got time to read and catch up with latest research, don't have time to write and explore new thinking etc. The advantage of this approach is that I may feel quite passionate and convinced, but it has many disadvantages from an influencing perspective. I may get a bit upset, I may sound accusing, my boss might get defensive etc.

If I look at it from taking a common perspective I will look into what my boss's position is. She may not have enough staff to cover my absence, and in any case it will be easy for her to refuse if I do not have clear arguments and present a case which benefits the organisation.

So what do we have in common? We both want Ashridge to have excellent world class seminars, we both want our professors to be excellent teachers and be up to date on the latest research. We both want Ashridge to be present in the publishing arena.

So I can start of my request by framing it in such a way that I am talking about the benefits to Ashridge, then to her, and only lastly to me. In every influencing situation you can try to look for what both parties have in common – sometimes this is very obvious, at other times you may have to do some research or be particularly creative.

What's in it for them (WIIFT)

Building on the above, an effective way of approaching your influencing situation is to ask – what's in it for them? If the answer is nothing then you are either going to have to be an awfully good influencer (or more likely manipulator) or give up trying to influence that particular audience on that subject. There *has* to be something in it for them. It may not be obvious and you may need to be quite creative, but you need to consider this strongly. So, what *could* be in it for them? or what *might* happen if they do *not* do this.

This means that before influencing a person or group you need to stop, reflect and actually ask yourself the question. If you do not find an answer here then you will not be effective in influencing. You can be creative and maybe you can find something in it for a person that they didn't know was in it for themselves. In fact being creative here is kind of essential because you can help people look at things differently and find things they didn't see (see section on reframing in chapter 6). This is what effective coaches also do.

Another side to WIIFT is the influencee asking the same question about you. When you are trying to sell them something or convince them of something, one of the first questions they will ask is what's in it for you? And they are likely to come up with an answer fairly quickly that looks something like – more money for you, more power, more prestige etc. So they will think that there is more in it for you – the seller, as it were, than there is for them, the buyer!

And if you haven't thought of what's in it for *them* you are going to have a problem!

If there is an imbalance – that is lots in it for you and not a lot in it for them, then you will not be effective. Of course there is usually going to be something in it for you, otherwise you wouldn't be trying to persuade them, but the important thing is to be honest and ethical about it. If you try to tell the other person that there is nothing in it for you, they are just not going to believe you. So be open, and try for a win-win outcome. If there is not a win-win outcome possible then either you aren't looking hard enough, you are not being creative enough, or you shouldn't be trying to influence someone. (And there are times when influence won't work and is not appropriate)

DEVELOPING SHARED VALUES

If you want to be successful at influencing, you must also take into account the values and beliefs of the person you wish to influence. If your desired outcome is not congruent with the other person's values, then you will not be able to influence them. You must be able to frame your outcome in a way that is congruent with their beliefs. Again, the first thing to do is find out just what their values and beliefs are, then frame your position accordingly.

However, we do not suggest that you pretend or lie. In many cases there will be congruence between your position and the other person's value system. If there is not, then either change your proposal or accept that you are unlikely to influence.

BRAIN DOMINANCE

Ned Hermann's Thinking Style Preference model is a useful one to be aware of when influencing others. He splits the brain into four quadrants – upper left and upper right, and lower left and lower right (1993).

The left side is associated with logic, analysis, organisation etc. – or 'hard' thinking while the right side is associated with intuition, emotional, interpersonal, or 'soft' thinking. The upper quadrant is cerebral (or head) thinking and the lower quadrant is called limbic (or body) mode.

In learning for example, the upper left person responds to formalised lectures, data based content and, technical case discussions. The lower left respond well to thorough planning, sequential order, lectures, structure etc.

The upper right person responds to spontaneity, being involved, future oriented case discussions, visual displays and experimentation. The lower right respond to group interaction, experiential opportunities and people oriented case discussions.

We can see this fairly clearly at Ashridge. My Hermann preference is right brained and I struggle with order, planning, details, logical sequences, and rigour. Many of the participants in our courses have a left brained preference and actually need to see order, logical flow, would like expert advice, tool boxes, answers etc. Sometimes there is a lack of communication – so unless I point out and make these preferences clear from the beginning we risk seeing the world from a different perspective. Often the feedback I will get from clients is that I am creative, enthusiastic, a good teacher yet unstructured, So if I want to be an effective influencer and communicator in the classroom I have to ensure at least a minimum amount of order and structure. This is far from easy – these preferences are often strongly ingrained and we can find it difficult to adapt and change even when we accept that we need to.

Hermann describes the quadrants in the following ways – which of these describes you best?

Upper left	Lower left	Lower right	Upper right
▶ Logical ▶ Factual ▶ Critical ▶ Rational ▶ Analytical ▶ Quantitative	Data collector Conservative Controlled Sequential Articulate Dominant Detailed	Musical Spiritual Symbolic Talkative Emotional Intuitive	Creative/innovative regarding solutions Simultaneous Synthesiser Holistic Artistic Spatial
They use phrases like 'Tools', Hardware, Bottom Line, and Critical analysis	They use phrases like 'Habits,' We have always done it this way, Self discipline, Sequence, by the book, play it safe,	They use phrases like Team work, Interactive, Participatory, Personal growth, Team development	They use phrases like play with an idea, big picture, broad based, cutting edge, conceptual, innovative

Tick the descriptors in each one and calculate which one is your preference. Now think of a person you typically have to influence (colleague, partner, boss) and try the same thing for them. Clearly people using words from the right side are not going to be influential for people who have a left brained preference. You need to reflect on your own preferences (Hermann suggests that most people have a double preference and that a small number have a preference for four).

Think about what that means for your communications. One of the authors tends to talk about ideas, creativity, big picture future, possibilities, energy, enthusiasm, and never about costs, sales, market share, profit, deadlines, detail etc. So if he is trying to influence someone who has a different brain preference, he may not be very effective!

Then think about the people you need to influence – where are they on the brain preference? How do they talk? What has meaning for them? How easy is it for you to start speaking their language? (Do not underestimate the difficulty here).

The above is just a short description of the preferences – we refer you to Herrman's Split Brain Dominance Instrument for an accurate description of your personal dominance profile.

Try it – think of a person at work who you have to influence regularly – listen to them over a period of time, ask them some questions. Write down the words and phrases they typically use. Then try to use some of these words back to them, For example if you gave an idea for a new product and you are a right brainer, don't talk about future and possibilities and people and ideas and holistic. Instead frame your thoughts in a way that makes sense to the other – tell them how your idea is practical, rigorous, backed up by research, will improve the bottom line, date etc.

Many of the great influencing speeches have huge emotional content in them. Listen for example to the speeches of Winston Churchill, Nelson Mandela, Martin Luther King, Bob Geldof, or similar people in the public eye in your country.

INFLUENCING ANGRY PEOPLE

If you are having to deal with angry people then the first rule is to Listen. The second rule is to Listen, and the third rule is to Listen some more. Listening helps drain the anger; trying to argue does not. Give them your attention and respect – listen to what they have to say. On no account try to tell them why they are wrong and you are right! (even if they are wrong) Allow them to get whatever it is off their chest – don't contradict them. Many people try to interrupt and resist the complaint. Don't interrupt. Don't resist the complaint. Don't give excuses. Don't get defensive. Listen! When they have calmed down, ask them what they would like you to do.

✍ SUMMARY OF KEY POINTS

Important elements of awareness of others relate mainly to *planning and preparing,* understanding in detail who the others are by fully examining all the relevant *stakeholders.*

You must take account of the various *power bases* of all the stakeholders, as well as understanding your own power in relation to the others.

Other areas to consider include:

☛ Searching for mutual perspective
☛ What's in it for them
☛ Developing shared values
☛ Brain preference

6 Approaches and Techniques

Using Your Toolkit

> *To accomplish great things, we must not only act, but also dream; not only plan, but also believe.*
>
> Anatole France 1844–1924. French writer

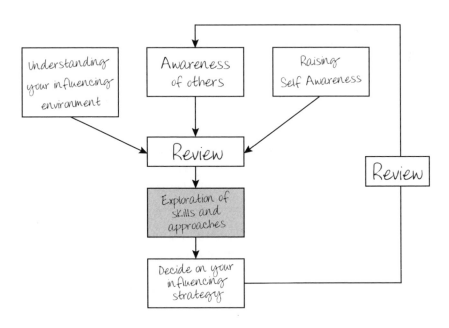

A MODEL FOR INFLUENCING

In this chapter we offer a number of tried and tested tools and techniques. No one of them will guarantee success but used with skill they will help you to become a more effective influencer.

Link and build

Linking your perspective and the other person's is one of the key levers for effective influencing. Too often we make no connections between what we are proposing and the other person's position, in fact we often don't know what the others position is …! First of all (as we have seen) you need to discover the others person's views, position and perspective. Once you have established that you then need to make a link – build a bridge in effect – between your position and their position. So in effect you are looking for whatever common ground you can.

In some cases that link might be strong and you just need to highlight the link that is already there. So metaphorically speaking the bridge is solid. In other cases that link will be more tenuous – more like a rope bridge than the Forth Bridge over the Forth Estuary in Scotland for example! You still have to build that bridge though, and make a link, however tenuous, between the positions and ideas.

Often in arguments we either accept or reject other's ideas. This is not effective in building rapport or in finding new creative ideas.

In fact what we need to be able to do is to pick out what you do like or what you do agree with in their position and restate that. Then build onto it, so for example instead of saying 'brilliant idea' or 'that's a rubbish idea' you say, 'What I like about your thinking is XXXXX *and* we can also consider YYYYYY'.

Most people do not expect their arguments or ideas to be 100 per cent correct and for everyone to accept them completely. But at the same time most people want to be listened to and taken seriously and not rejected out of hand. By linking and building you create rapport, show others that you are listening and taking them seriously, avoid defensiveness and generate better solutions.

Of course sometimes you may have to look pretty closely at their idea to find something you can build on, but be creative, tell them you like their commitment or passion or enthusiasm if you don't like the idea itself.

Remember you are not likely to be 100 per cent correct all of the time either, so, don't be afraid to compromise.

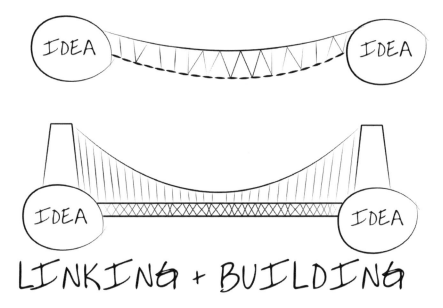

The art of framing and reframing

> *Truth is not what we discover, but what we create*
> Antoine de St. Exupery

Reframing is changing the way you perceive an event thereby changing the meaning. When you change the meaning, responses and behaviour will also change. According to American psychologist Paul Watlawick (1980), to reframe means to alter the conceptual and/or emotional setting or viewpoint in relation to which a situation is experienced. The experience is placed in another, different frame which fits the facts of the situation as well, or even better, thus changing its (the situation's) meaning completely. As Shakespeare said, 'There is nothing good or bad, but thinking makes it so' (*Hamlet* Act II Scene 2).

A good example of reframing is given in Chapter Two of Mark Twain's novel '*The Adventures of Tom Sawyer*'. The hero, Tom Sawyer is prevented from playing with his friends because he has to whitewash a fence. One of his friends, Ben Rogers, comes along and teases him. Sawyer has an inspiration. He says that it is not a chore, in fact it's really enjoyable;

'Why, ain't that work?' says Ben.

'Well maybe it is and maybe it ain't. all I know is it suits Tom Sawyer' replies Tom.

'Oh come now, you don't mean to let on that you LIKE it?' says Ben.

And Tom replies that he doesn't see why he oughtn't to like it. After all a boy doesn't get a chance to whitewash a fence every day!

Tom then steps back to admire his handiwork. He adds an effect here, a touch there, pretends to be completely absorbed in his painting.

A few moments later Ben asks him if he can do some whitewashing! Sawyer says that he cannot, because his aunt, who gave him the task, is very particular about who could do it. Only one boy in a thousand, maybe two thousand could do it the way it has to be done. A moment later and Ben offers to give him his apple if only Tom will allow him to do the whitewashing!

Sawyer has reframed what was seen as a chore into something interesting and pleasurable, and in the process of doing so has influenced his friend to do the chore for him.

Later Mark Twain has Tom reflect on this, and he says that in order to make a man or boy covet something, all you have to do is make the thing difficult to obtain. He goes on to write about the difference between work and play. He realises that it is a question of framing:

Work he says, consists of what someone is *obliged* to do, and play is whatever someone is not obliged to do. If you are able to frame your work as something you are not obliged to do, but do it because you want to do it, it gives a very different outcome.

Another excellent example of reframing is the reaction of the King Christian of Denmark in 1943 when the Nazi emissary asked him how he intended to solve the Jewish problem. The King replied, 'We do not have a Jewish problem, *we* do not feel inferior'. The King also went on to reframe the situation when the Nazis issued a decree stating that all Jews had to wear a yellow armband with the Star of David on it, thus making it easy for Nazis to identify Jewish people. He said that all Danes were the same and therefore all Danes would wear the armband, and he himself would be the first to wear it.

There are two main types of reframe – context reframe and content reframe.

CONTEXT REFRAME

When you hear a complaint of the type, 'I am too lazy ...' or 'that person is too stubborn ...', the person complaining is taking away context or is putting the behaviour in a context where it is a disadvantage.

You can change this by asking in what context/circumstances would the behaviour have value or be seen as positive?

EXAMPLE

If you know someone who you think is obsessive about details, you could describe them in the following way;
   'Jenny is obsessive about details.'
   Now this is not particularly flattering, and if Jenny were to describe herself she might choose to put this in a different frame and say;
   'I am a bit of a perfectionist!'
   This alters how people would perceive the meaning of the phrase. So it is clearly a useful technique when you wish to influence others.

If you think of someone as 'stubborn', you can reframe this as, 'this person is an idealist'. Now if you want to create a relationship with the person (maybe he/she is your boss for example) it will be a lot easier to develop a positive relationship if you frame the person as idealist and act accordingly. You can further reframe idealist into strong minded, which will alter your perception of their actions and your reactions and behaviour.

Often we are too quick to frame from a particular perspective in the first place. We see someone being a bit critical and we can then label them as obsessive or narrow minded, and then interpret every action they take after that as negative. Perhaps they were just having a bad day, or they were feeling a bit defensive about something.

CONTENT REFRAME

You can use content reframing when you don't like your reaction to an event. For example if you have to buy a smaller car than you wanted to, your frame is likely to be your neighbours' thoughts about you, your friend's reactions, your self image etc. (Your internal dialogue may be, 'I am not successful enough ...')

What you can do is to reframe the content. So the reframe will go like this, 'I will save a fortune on petrol and insurance', 'It is less harmful to the environment', 'I live in a big city and it will be so much more practical to park' etc.

You can apply content reframes when you are influencing others. So if you are selling a fairly undesirable car – let's say you have a fairly old, small, battered car from a country which is not reputed for the quality of its cars. At first sight you would imagine this would be difficult to sell – because the potential buyers are already framing it as old, battered, small, under-powered, undesirable etc. What you can do to be more influential and try to persuade them to at least consider your car is to reframe the content to a more desirable one. In this case you can reframe small as 'easy to park', or easy to handle around town.

You can reframe the fact that it is a bit dented as 'it is unlikely to be stolen' or 'every car in the city gets scratched and dented – a few more scratches on this one won't make any difference'. You can reframe underpowered as 'very economical – high miles per gallon', or point out that average speed within London for example is 12 mph, so you won't need a high powered car! In fact the car is starting to sound like the ideal car for the cost conscious city dweller. I have a friend who lives in Avignon in France, who is proud of the fact that her ancient battered Citroen is perfect for that city as hardly a week goes by without the car being scratched or bumped. If she had a shiny new car she'd constantly be having to take it to the garage, and anyway it would probably have been stolen! So by reframing her thinking about her car, she is more able to resist the urge to buy a bright and shiny new car, and also better equipped to resist the jibes of her friends who criticise her for driving around in an old wreck.

Paul Watzlawick gives another good example of reframing. A couple's parents were always buying things, coming over, taking over, and clean-ing the couple's house. The couple felt as if they were being treated as kids by the parents and it was putting a strain on their relationship. They tried to clean up and buy stuff in before the parents came over, but to no avail. No matter what they did the parents were still finding things wrong. At the end of their tether they went for counselling to Watzlawick.

Watzlawick reframes the situation and tells them *not* to buy food, *not* to clean or tidy. They find this difficult, but force themselves to act as slobs, not to do any shopping, not to offer to help the parents in law, just to relax and let the parents in law do all the shopping and cleaning. Faced with this situation the parents get so fed up that they leave – telling the couple that they are now adults and old enough to look after themselves, so they should grow up. An effective outcome – so very influential.

A word of warning. Be careful not to get into compulsive and inap-propriate reframes. If someone has their car stolen the appropriate reac-tion is sympathy followed by offers of practical help, not unhelpful reframes such as: 'Think of the exercise and fresh air you will get' or 'You'll be able to experience now how poor people without cars live.'

OTHER USEFUL FRAMES ...

Outcome rather than blame

When we are annoyed, angry or upset about something, or with some-one, we often end up blaming them for their part in the situation. This might be cathartic for you but it does not take you forward. The person being blamed is likely to become defensive, so they will not be motivated to help you resolve the issue at hand. Of course there are times when people deserve your annoyance, but that still will not help you resolve the issue. So what can you do? First of all, you will need to control your annoyance and your temper. Ok, we know they are to blame, but think! How will your anger help you to achieve your desired outcome? The answer is – it won't! So you will have to focus on something else other than blame. And that something else is the outcome you want to achieve.

What behaviour will best serve the achievement of your outcome? Studies have shown that one of the key derailers of top managers is lack of impulse control. So control your immediate impulse and focus on what it is you want to achieve. Then focus on *how* you might achieve that. If you have people around you who like being blamed then fine – go ahead and use blame! But for the huge majority of people this will not work. We are not saying that you cannot be angry; appropriate anger is fine – as long as you can tell someone you are angry without showing the anger! Because as soon as you show it you will get defensiveness. The capacity to share your feelings without necessarily losing control of your feelings is key.

Possibilities rather than necessities

Doing something because one *has* to do it is not motivating or terribly influential. Looking at what is possible can often go beyond what has to be done and is more involving. If you reframe what *has* to be done into what *could* be done, then you are likely to appeal to people's creativity and energy. It's the same for yourself. Ask yourself what is possible for you to do, rather than 'What do I have to do?' Saying 'have to' is an instant turn off!

Many people frame their perspective on work by asking themselves what is not possible. They say things like 'I could never do that,' 'that's impossible'. If you look at all the things that are not possible then you are going to get an awful long list! Turn it round – ask yourself, and others what *is*, or *might*, be possible.

Feedback rather than failure

Do not think of an event where you did not get what you want as 'Failure' as so many people do. We think that labelling a performance as failure is a disaster in terms of influence and motivation. Too often we label situations in terms of win – lose. They won, we lost! It is really not helpful. If someone gets the job we wanted for example, how does it help to say 'I lost'? Better to explore why we did not get the job, asking for feedback and explanations. Then take on board the feedback, make some changes and move forwards. So next time you, your team, or your company doesn't get what you want, don't just lament the fact, or worse still blame others or yourself for that matter.

Get specific feedback, take it on board and you will find that you are in a better, more resourceful state to learn and progress.

Curiosity rather than assumptions

We can often be guilty of making assumptions. It's natural but it's not helpful. In our work we often have to challenge managers by asking them if what they say is a known fact or merely an assumption on their part. So when you find yourself making sweeping statements – check and ask your self if this is really not just an assumption. While you're at it, run a check through all of the assumptions you are holding – 'my team is lazy', 'my boss enjoys making me work long hours', 'the client is difficult', 'these participants are being deliberately awkward'.

Replace assumptions with curiosity, ask more questions. Keep an open mind. Probe, discover, ask open not closed questions. Be genuinely curious.

Sometimes, when I am playing golf and leading by a lot (this doesn't happen often) I get lazy and my opponent starts catching up. I then tend to get depressed and pessimistic and feel that I will lose the game from here on (in reality I am still leading, but my frame of mind is I'm losing). Then I start to play badly and end up really losing the game. So I need to stop for a second, focus and then reframe that *I am* winning, therefore I am better, can play golf and should go on to win this game!

In conclusion, the ability to master the Art of Reframing is essential if you are to be an effective and successful influencer.

Exercise

Take a situation you are in, that you are experiencing difficulty with, and have a go at reframing the situation (you can ask a partner, friends and colleagues to reframe the situation for you as well).

Explain the situation as you see it, then deliberately look at it from other perspectives and different frames. Do not make judgements at this stage. Simply try to view the situation in another way, perhaps using the techniques outlined above. You will find that this will give you much more flexibility and creativity in your influencing approach. Ask your partner or colleagues to challenge you to see the situation in as many frames and perspectives as possible.

Ask and listen

At first sight asking and listening doesn't appear to be influencing. You tend to think that you should be telling or arguing in order to be an effective influencer but it's just not true. Because influencing is a process you need to create rapport with and generate valuable information by discovering the other person's perspective. Once you know the facts and emotions you can recognise their point of view and then build on it or reframe your perspective in order for it to be better accepted by the other. This means that the skills of questioning, probing and listening need to be mastered.

We cannot emphasise enough how important it is for you to find out where the other person is coming from and then build your persuasive case around them. This does not mean giving up your own perspective, but it *does* mean that you have to be flexible, and this is easier said than done. What is stopping you from being flexible? How attached are you to your own perspective or being right? You do need to take a long hard look at yourself here, and genuinely reflect on how you might be less flexible than you need to be to be an effective influencer.

Shared rewards

When you attempt to influence someone, the first thing you probably think of is what *you* want. Typically you think of what your goal is, what you want to achieve, then try to find arguments to convince the other person. In other words you are thinking of the rewards you will get. Let's turn this on its head. Instead of thinking about what you want, ask rather what the rewards are for the other person if they do what you want them to do.

If these rewards are obvious, like more money, recognition, promotions, more free time, less stress, more chance of success, for example, then it will not be too difficult to convince them. If on the other hand, you don't actually see any rewards for them, you have a problem! This is where you need to push your thinking, or change your goal, so that there are clear rewards for the other person. Remember it is very likely that what they consider as a reward might differ from yours. Its like the story of sharing an orange; we assume that the fair way to do that is to cut it in half. But, if one person wants the juice, and the other wants the rind (for cooking/baking for instance) then cutting it in half is a lose-lose situation. The point being that you should first ask what they want to do with the orange.

The language of influence

Do you remember what it's like when you go to the dentist? If you are like me you will have horrible memories of dentists' waiting rooms as a kid. But, have you noticed the language the dentist uses to influence their patients? When something hurts and they haven't warned you beforehand that it's going to hurt a lot, but have told you that you will feel 'slight pressure', or a 'slight lab'. If they did tell you it would hurt like hell, you'd just tense up, make their job more difficult and it would hurt even more because you expected it to hurt.

It's like chefs talking about steak. Where you and I see a fatty bit of meat, they will talk about 'marbled beef'.

So naming something has a massive effect on influencing. A telephone sales person asks for just a few seconds of your time, or they say 'we are not selling anything', just getting some information. The double glazing representative calls to tell you 'I'm not selling you anything Mr Brent, just letting you know we are working in your area this week'.

NEGATIVE LANGUAGE

Psychologists tell us that the difference between a happy marriage and a failed marriage is that in the happy one the partners use positive language to each other five times more than they use negative language. So if you want to influence effectively try to use more positive language in your relationships. Negative language is very powerful – I like to get praise as much as the next person, but when I get negative feedback, for example in a seminar, I can remember that for years! It also makes me feel terrible and the interesting thing is that one piece of negative feedback can out punch 20 pieces of positive feedback. So be very careful with your use of negative language – especially in relationships and where you have absolutely no formal authority (be especially careful then).

For example, one of our colleagues had just delivered a training session and another colleague had observed the session; his feedback about the delivery was 'That was really boring!' On receiving this feedback our colleague became very defensive – a not uncommon response to such negative language. So he was not actually positively influenced by the remarks. A better way of influencing would have been to make a positive comment on the content, which was new and interesting, and to have said that it would have been even more interesting if it had involved more exercises and discussion with the audience. We have actively tried this approach and find that people are more open to change when you frame your feedback in a positive way.

Appreciative inquiry

Appreciative Inquiry is a technique which has evolved since its beginnings in the USA in the early 80s. It is a technique that we feel can be used very effectively as a way of involving and influencing others, in a non directive and ethical way. Maybe we should say it is a way of facilitating people to influence themselves! It is the opposite of a *push* or *directive* style of influencing, and is a tool that managers should be able to use if they are to manage their people and organisations effectively, using their peoples' own energy, thoughts and motivations.

As a young doctoral student at Case Western Reserve University in the USA, David Cooperrider did an organisational analysis for the Cleveland Clinic. He was trying to find out what was wrong with the human side of the organisation. During his investigation he was amazed and excited at the level of cooperation he was getting from the staff. His supervisor Suresh Srivasta noticed this enthusiasm and suggested that he make that enthusiasm and excitement the object of the inquiry. So Cooperrider analysed the factors contributing, not to failure, but to the effective functioning of the clinic. This work in the early 80s developed into a technique called Appreciative Inquiry (AI). The technique involves inquiring into what works, what is effective in an organisation, rather than the classical problem solving approach of delving into all the problems the organisation is facing. They discovered that by focussing on what was good, they were able to increase performance and morale in their original study at the Clinic. Research also showed that the employees' rate of learning increased.

The tools and techniques have evolved over the years and there is now a large body of research into these techniques. The basis though, remains the same – Appreciative Inquiry focuses on what is good, what is working, what is effective in an organisation. The basic philosophy is that what you focus your attention on grows. To put it simplistically, if you focus your attention on what is not working, and what is wrong, then you are likely to get bogged down in all the things that are not working, and at the same time, miss all the things that are working well!

It is the opposite of deficit based model of change. It does not see a situation as a problem to be fixed, but rather a new opportunity or new possibility. With AI, you look back at what has worked in the past, in order to then look forward to what could be possible.

How does this link to effective Influencing? Think about a time when you have faced a problem or issue with a colleague, boss or subordinate. How have you typically gone about dealing with it? If you are like many of the managers who we talk to, you may have tried to focus on the issue, let the other person know why you are not happy, then go on to tell them what they could do about it. In other words, we take a deficit approach to the issue. This of course may work, but it does tend to create resistance. The first reaction we all tend to have when criticised is to get defensive.

If you adopt a modified AI approach, then what you can do is before focusing on all the problems and areas where you are being let down, focus on what the other person (or team or department) actually does well.

Ah, we hear you say, they don't do anything well – that's the problem! In fact that is unlikely, and if they really don't do anything well, you have been in denial for a long time! On reflection you'll probably admit that the person is pretty good at some things. For instance they may be reliable, good at detail, dependable, etc. Your issue may be, for example, that they never take the initiative. It will be a lot easier to influence this person if they are not angry and defensive. The technique then, is to recognise what *is* working, to tell the person what you appreciate about their work and attitude, and then ask how they might go about taking more initiative (if that is the issue). Even if you do feel forced to give them some so called constructive feedback, he or she will probably be in a better state to receive it if you have done them the courtesy of recognising that they are in fact good at many things.

We describe this as a modified AI style because AI would only focus on the positive aspects. As Watkins and Mohr describe it, AI is based on the belief that humans will show a tendency to move toward positive images. We do not go so far, but believe that as an influencing technique, the appreciative approach can work wonders. It often amazes us when we see the energy generated by using such an appreciative approach. A simple recognition of what someone is doing well puts them in a better frame of mind to accept feedback and dispose them to listen to your perspective.

One of the key elements of being a successful influencer is surely that the other person must listen to what you have to say. Criticism and blame are hardly likely to encourage others to do so.

On the other hand we are saddened by the frequent use of the deficit based approach by practising managers. Even if managers do not actively use this deficit approach, they often simply miss out the positives! As an example, one of the authors ran a leadership development seminar for a multi national company in China. There was no official feedback from the company as to how this seminar had gone. The company had paid the author very promptly and there had been unofficial feedback from one of the participants that the training had been a success, but no word from the client. We are an insecure profession and like to know when things go well! On another seminar with different participants we met the client and asked him how the China session had gone. His reply was that if we hadn't heard from them it must have been fine! The conclusion was that this company didn't think it was important to tell a trainer or consultant the good news that his or her seminar or intervention had gone well. The only feedback would be if things went wrong!

I asked the client if this was typical and he answered that it was pretty typical of the company's culture. Managers expected little praise, just blame if things went wrong. The attitude was that it's normal that you do your job well – that's what you get paid for!!

So we feel that this particular company would do well to use the AI technique a bit more and start to also focus and recognise when people do things well. It is a heck of a lot more energising and motivating than blame or criticism. If the only time you give your people attention is to blame them then they are going to start avoiding you, or worse, start doing things wrong just to get some attention!

EXAMPLE

You have someone in your team who is excellent at the functional and technical aspects of their job but who is poor at the communication and people side. Someone who is perhaps timid, lacks confidence and is somewhat introverted.

You really need them to communicate more effectively and be more of a team leader. You are unwilling to fire them as they are technically excellent, motivated, helpful and are no trouble. Still, you are scratching your head as to what to do about him/her. You have tried to tell them to be more confident, less introverted, but this hasn't worked. On the contrary they seemed to retreat into their shell and got upset when you did that.

So what do you do? Ordering someone to be more confident is like telling someone to be more spontaneous. It just doesn't work. How can AI help? What AI assumes is that this person, as a normal functioning adult, will have demonstrated confidence, initiative, assertiveness, communication ability at some time in their lives. So as a manager or coach, you begin to ask, to inquire into when the person has felt confident for example. Maybe they dealt with a family situation confidently, maybe they were assertive in a sports team at school, or dealing with areas they knew about. So now you inquire into what helped them to behave in that way, what were they doing? What did they feel? What did they say? How were others reacting?

Then you ask the person how they can use these skills and resources which they have used before, in the future. What resources can they bring to bear on the situation at work for example. This approach influences others – it moves them forward, it gives them resources to deal with situations. It equips them to handle situations which they did not think they were able to handle. It looks for the resources they have in themselves and builds on them.

Create a compelling case

You still need to be able to convince others and a weak unprepared unstructured argument won't do it. Neither will just repeating facts or the plaintiff cry of 'But I'm right'. So do your homework and follow the points below to create a compelling argument.

FACTS

Although many people are swayed by emotions and feelings more than facts most people will need the basic facts. So do your research, find out as many facts as you can and above all get back up from other sources. Don't just say '*I* think' or '*I* believe'. Nobody really cares what you think! Tell us that the National Council for Research's (or whatever) national inquiry into X discovered three key facts.

Which of the following do you find more influential?

'I think smoking is terrible'.

Or

The National Health Commission's research into heart disease found that 50 per cent of smokers die before they are 60??

Most people would be more convinced by the latter argument! Don't give too many facts though or you will bore your audience to tears. If they are fact feeders give them additional information to read or give references they can pick up on, otherwise stick to three key facts.

CREATIVITY

Many people who need to influence regularly have not thought that they need to be creative – they think that it's enough for them to believe and to simply present the arguments.

As Bill Bernbach, a New York advertising executive said (quoted in Paul Arden, 2003):

> The truth isn't the truth until people believe you, and they can't believe you if they don't know what you are saying, and they can't know what you are saying if they don't listen to you, and they won't listen to you if you're not interesting, and you won't be interesting unless you say things, imaginatively, originally, freshly.

He is absolutely right! Be different! Use images, symbols, metaphors – make your argument stand out from the crowd.

Bill Bryson (2003) has a great example in his book, *A Short History of Everything* – he asks you to consider the amount of time the world has existed for. You can say something like 4550000000 years – which lets face it, is pretty meaningless to most of us.

Or

You ask some one to stand with their arms outstretched and give a colleague a nail file. You ask the colleague to file the edge of the person's nail – There! You have just filed off the whole of recorded history!

Which is likely to stay in the memory longer?

He also tells us that there are perhaps 140 billion galaxies in the universe. How can you imagine such a number? Bryson helps us out again by writing that if galaxies were peas, that would be enough to fill the Royal Albert Hall.

METAPHORS

Creativity is a key aspect of influencing. As Einstein said, there is nothing that is a more certain sign of insanity than to do the same thing over and over again and expect the results to be different! 'Fail, fail again, fail better', said Samuel Beckett.

Paul Arden in his great little book *Its Not How Good You Are Its How Good You Want To Be*, gives a telling example of how we can be perceived by others. He shows a business card with the words:

ANTONY TAYLOR
ARCHITECT

then on the other side of the page:

ANTONY TAYLOR
ARCHITECTS

Which is the most influential? In our opinion Architects gives an extra dimension of permanence, competence and professionalism. All done by simply adding an *S*.

MAKE IT SEXY

Irish rock star Bono has a well publicised campaign to stop poverty in Africa. In the past the way it was presented was to show the effects of poverty; the influence of this type of campaign was designed more to pull at people's heart strings, or make them feel guilty and therefore give money. But nowadays there are so many charities vying for our money and attention. Bono realised that they would have to approach it in a different, more creative way – he says that this was show business, that they were creating drama 'We were very conscious that in order to prevail on Africa we would have to get better at dramatising the situation so we could make Africa less of a burden and more of an adventure." (*Guardian* Interview – 16 June 2005)

How are you approaching your influencing situation? How can you dramatise it more? How can you make it more of an adventure?

IMAGES SYMBOLS AND METAPHORS

This is a key area in terms of being creative in your influencing. In our influencing course we ask participants to draw/paint a picture of the issue they are facing and a picture of their vision of what could be. Typically we have some initial resistance by some participants who think that drawing a picture is kiddie school stuff. Others immediately tell us they can't draw, can't paint and are not creative (they are usually the people who come up with the best stuff!) But using images unlocks creativity and thoughts that were not available beforehand. Further, it paints a picture for the influence and stays much longer in other's minds than mere words.

The picture we ask for is typically the situation now and the vision of where you want to get to. You can do it in two or three steps – where you are now, where you want it to be (the bright picture) and possibly where you will be if things continue as they are (the dark picture).

The drawing above is an example taken from one of our participants in Italy. It represents the situation the department is facing at the moment.

This is from the same participant but is the vision of where she would like the department to be in the future.

Not only did this help her to visualise exactly how she felt about the current situation but it helped her to imagine clearly what she wanted to achieve, and to share that vision with her team.

The drawing below is by one of the participants on the Ashridge seminar. Before doing the visioning exercise he had spoken about how his company wasted a lot of money, but he had not done this in a particularly gripping or interesting way. He used lots of numbers and facts but the others in the group were not strongly influenced by his presentation. After doing the exercise he came up with the vision below. Now he, and we, could picture the situation much more easily. The company was like a giant tap, with huge amounts of money just dripping away. Each drip represents money, the wastage, the effect on the people etc. So although the drawing is not particularly artistic, it achieves the goal of giving a strong visual image to the situation and enables the influencer to make graphic representations in the minds of their audience.

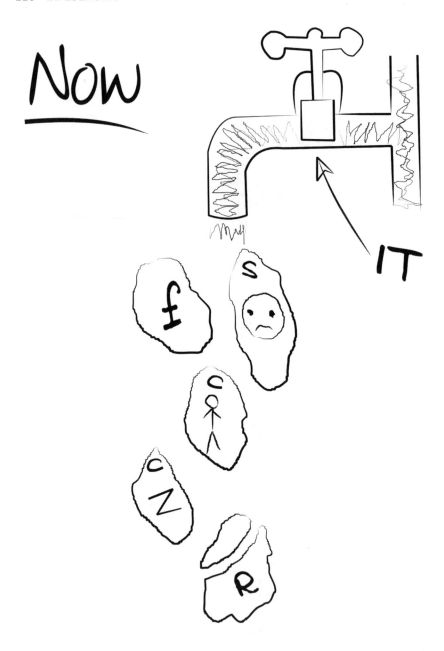

Interestingly we meet a lot of resistance during this part of the seminar –
our participants tell us that this is Mickey Mouse/kids stuff and that it is
not useful! But think for a moment of the potency of some of the symbols
we live with. Think of the thoughts you associate with a crucifix, or a star
of David, or a crescent shape or your national flag. Now think of someone
burning this symbol. In many countries burning or defacing the flag is a

criminal offence; in some countries defacing a religious symbol would get you killed. I don't think of myself as particularly religious or nationalistic but I have to recognise the effect of some symbols in my life. Being Scottish I am happy when I see the flag of St Andrews flying in Edinburgh on public buildings, being of Jewish origin I get upset and angry if I see a Swastika. I am struck each time I visit Sweden by the enormous number of homes which fly the Swedish flag.

So symbols have power and meaning and you can use them in both positive and negative ways in your influencing. For example if you wanted to paint a dark picture of what would happen if we allowed Fascism to become strong in the UK, you ask people to imagine a Swastika flying over the Houses of Parliament (of course this would only be a meaningful vision to those people who really knew what the Swastika represents).

In an interesting article in *Business Week*, D. Leonhardt and K. Kerwin tell us that in the USA many children recognise the MacDonald's symbol – the Yellow Arches – before they are 20 months old (*Business Week*, 30 June 1997). So you can use symbols in your presentations and influencing scenarios to shock, to have strong impact, to make them more dramatic and more memorable.

RELATE EMOTIONALLY

It seems that in organisations logic is more valued than emotions. Again many of our participants show a clear preference to be logical rather than emotional – preferring to be like Mr Spock in Star Trek rather than the more emotional Bones. When you agree with someone you tend to consider them as logical, but if you disagree then what happens is that you say the argument is illogical or emotional. One of my previous bosses in France once said to me, 'The problem with you Brent is that you are emotional'. So it was not ok to be emotional; logic was valued and rewarded and signs of emotion discouraged. Of course there may be a theme in French manufacturing companies of valuing logic but this is something both of us have often noticed in the companies and organisations we work with.

The challenge is to use both logic and emotions appropriately. *Logic on its own is not enough!* Many of our participants tell us that they know they are right but that they cannot get people to agree with them. The fact is they may well be right, but being right is not enough. This comes as a bit of a shock though, as these people have been brought up in the belief that being right *is* enough. So even if you are right, think how you can use emotion as well. Try to connect with the other person or people, use empathy and respect their perspective.

It is extremely difficult to persuade someone who believes in something emotionally to change their minds if you only argue logically. If I believe in Jesus Christ then logical argument is not going to work to persuade me that He doesn't exist. My faith is not going to be shaken by logic because my faith is not logical – it is about belief.

However the truth is that we are emotional creatures as well as logical ones so it is important to connect at an emotional level as well as a logical one.

Just Do it (JDI)

At first glance JDI sounds like a strange tool in Influencing. Our experience is that many people who think they should influence do not actually even try very hard to do it. The manager of a large hypermarket in France told me that many of her customers didn't actually complain when some thing went wrong. They would tell her about it months after the event when it was too late to do anything about it. She also said that most of the complaints she did receive did not include any specific influencing tactics – so for example a customer would come in and complain about some aspect of the goods or service *but that was all they would do – simply complain*! There was no mention of what she could do to redress the situation. Often the customer would come in, complain then walk out again. The manager was happy to give refunds or a free bottle of wine etc. to placate the customer but the fact is they rarely asked for anything.

So the first rule is if you don't ask you rarely get. And it is amazing what you can get if you simply ask. Another example, while I have been at home writing this book, I got a call from 3G mobiles. They offered me a brand new 3G handset, plus 500 any network anytime minutes and 100 text messages for the all inclusive price of £30 a month. I use the mobile phone a lot as I travel regularly and it sounded interesting. I checked my current suppliers' deal and found I was paying £25 a month for 200 minutes and with a fairly old phone. So no contest then in terms of value for money – 3G were far ahead. But of course there is a hassle involved in getting a new phone from a new company.

You have to change suppliers, networks, sim card, lose your old telephone number or go through a fairly complex routine to keep your old one, transferring all the numbers which were on your old phone's memory to the new phone's one – so there is some incentive to do nothing and just keep with old supplier. I was interested however to see if I could influence my old supplier and get a better deal with them. I phoned them up this morning, expecting to have to use a number of skills and techniques to persuade them. No such luck – I phoned them up, told them that 3G were offering a better deal and within 5 seconds my suppliers told me that she could match 3G, and send me a brand new phone to boot. It took me all of 30 seconds over all to get a matching deal. All I did was pick up the phone – but my supplier didn't phone me and ask me if I wanted a better deal. I had to get off my butt and do it. But that's all I had to do – simply ask. So many people I know don't bother to ask – they tell themselves stories about what would happen, that it would not work. But they don't even try!

People tell us about their situations at work and at home and how they would like to influence their colleagues or team or whatever, then we ask them what they have done so far – it is amazing how many people say they haven't done a thing 'I don't dare to ask' or 'it wouldn't work' 'but have you asked? Ah, well, no, not yet …'. So although you may need to use some of the other tools, techniques and strategies in this book – and of course HOW you ask is important – if you don't use this one first, you will not be very successful.

Have a clear idea of what you want, have a fall back position and then go for it. So if your flowers from the supermarket fade after two days, take them back and simply tell the clerk that you want your money back and a fresh bunch of flowers and that will resolve the inconvenience of disappointing whoever you bought the flowers for, yourself and the hassle of having to come back to the store. The manager might only offer you money back but bring in the emotional upset caused and the time and inconvenience caused too and be specific!

Influencing Staircase

Many people try to influence with out realising it is a process. Imagine a sort of influencing staircase – you must get agreement at each level of the argument. You must not assume agreement, as many managers we observe in fact do. If you are proposing something, check with everyone in the meeting that they do in fact agree. Don't just listen for words of agreement, look at their body language. If they look like they don't agree, check it out. It's a golden opportunity. Many managers pass over disagreement; they are scared of it. So they plough on regardless, then 30 minutes later are surprised when they don't have the total commitment of the people in the room; we have seen managers propose something, mutter 'ok' to themselves, keep their head down and avoid eye contact with anyone, and then blithely assume they have influenced the group and reached agreement!

Take it a step at a time, if you propose something (hopefully having asked for and built on the others' contributions). Stop, Shut up. look at the others. Ask 'are you ok on this'?, look at everyone in turn, get a verbal ok, or a nod. If anyone disagrees or even looks doubtful, check it out. ask them what they are thinking – don't ignore them or pretend they agree when they don't. It's a cardinal sin when influencing.

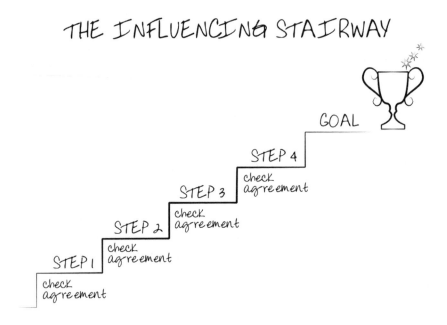

THE INFLUENCING STAIRWAY

GOAL

STEP 4
check agreement

STEP 3
check agreement

STEP 2
check agreement

STEP 1
check agreement

check agreement

Influencing in Shakespeare

We can learn much from Shakespeare on the subject of influencing and communication. You might object and ask how relevant he is today? In his book, *The Canon of the Western World*, the literary critic and Yale Professor, Harold Bloom, claims that Shakespeare invented psychoanalysis! Basically he is saying that Shakespeare discovered the unconscious before Freud and Jung …! What is undisputed is that Shakespeare shows great psychological insight, especially concerning leaders.

Shakespeare was the first person to use the word manager in the English language and Shakespeare expert Peter Dawkins writes that Shakespeare was also a great teacher and philosopher: 'Not only is Shakespeare a great poet, dramatist, neoplatonic philosopher and Christian Cabalist, but he is also a supreme teacher who teaches through entertainment following the path of the ancients.'

Shakespeare invented many of the words and expressions which we take for granted and still use today. Melvyn Bragg reckons he invented or recorded for the first time, over 2000 words and phrases, so in a way Shakespeare is still influencing our language.

Some of the expressions that we owe to him are:

▶ 'salad days',
▶ 'In my mind's eye',
▶ 'baby eyes',
▶ 'Smooth faced',
▶ 'what the dickens',
▶ 'in one fell swoop',
▶ 'vanish into thin air',
▶ 'all our yesterdays',
▶ 'more in sorrow than in anger',

and countless more.

Richard Olivier tells us that Shakespeare survives because he touches so consistently on the truth of human experience. Mark Rylance, actor and former director of the Globe Theatre, argues in his introduction to Olivier's book that leaders in society were always an audience in Shakespeare's mind, and says, 'I think he wanted the audience to understand themselves (whilst enjoying themselves) and he thought that theatre was the best way of doing that'.

In their book, *The Experience Economy*, Pine and Gilmore argue that work is theatre and every business a stage – if this is indeed the case, then clearly we can learn lessons, as managers, from the experience of playwrights, directors and actors. After all, we have to play a number of different roles in our work life.

The subject of Influence comes up time and again in Shakespeare. Let's look at extracts from one of his most famous plays, *Henry V*.

In *Henry V* Shakespeare has his hero use some of the most influential language when he influences the governor and citizens of Harfleur in France to surrender and then later in the famous St Crispins day speech to his soldiers.

Henry does not want to get stuck in Harfleur. He wants to march on to Calais, and cannot afford to stay in Harfleur besieging the town. He must influence the Governor of the town to lay down arms and surrender:

Therefore to our best mercy give yourselves
Or, like to men proud of destruction,
Defy us to do our worst; for, as I am a soldier,

A name that in my thoughts becomes me best,
If I begin the battr'y once again,
I will not leave the half achieved Harfleur
Till in her ashes she lies buried.
The gates of mercy shall be all shut up,
And the flesh'd soldier, rough and hard of heart,
In liberty of bloody hand shall range
With conscience wide as hell, mowing like grass
Your fresh fair virgins and your flow'ring infants.
What is it then to me if impious war,
Array'd in flames, like to the prince of fiends,
Do, with his smirch'd complexion, all fell feats
Enlink'd to waste and desolation?

Here Shakespeare uses all sorts of influencing devices – from alliteration to metaphor, powerful language and images. He implies that he cannot be responsible for the actions of his soldiers unleashed in a war that is more powerful than their consciences! His imagery is startling and creative – the image of his soldiers with bloody hand, mowing like grass their fair virgins and flowering infants is hugely impactful.

What is it to me when you yourselves are cause,
If your pure maidens fall into the hand
Of hot and forcing violation?
What rein can hold licentious wickedness
When down the hill he holds his fierce career?

He comes back to the image of what the townspeople hold dear – their young daughters – and exaggerates the image of what will happen, making it clear and graphic. He also puts the blame directly on them and not himself and his soldiers – if this happens then its their own fault! They have the option to surrender after all!

Therefore you men of Harfleur
take pity on of your town and of your people
Whiles yet my soldiers are at my command
Whiles yet the cool and temperate wind of grace
O'erblows the filthy and contagious clouds
Of heady murder, spoil and villany.

He appeals to them as well as threatening them; he implies again that it's not his fault but rather theirs. He compares the language of destruction and lack of control with the 'cool and temperate wind of grace' but tells them that this can only be short lived and that he is struggling to contain his men;

> *if not,-why in a moment look to see*
> *The blind and bloody soldier with foul hand*
> *Defile the locks of your shrill shrieking daughters*
> *Your fathers taken by the silver beards*
> *And their most revered heads dash'd to the walls*
> *Your naked infants spitted upon pikes*
> *Whiles the mad mothers with their howls confused*
> *Do break the clouds ... ...*

He leaves them in no doubt that this is going to happen and very soon. Yet again he comes back to what will happen to what is most precious – their daughters, but this time adds in for good measure their babies and their elders. It is not a case of simply saying 'We will kill your children' – he conjures up extremely graphic images, leaving nothing to the imagination and the effect is all the more powerful. One of the common shortcomings that managers have when they are trying to influence others is their over reliance on logic. Logic is usually not enough, and you have to appeal to the emotions and the right side of the brain.

Using creativity and imagination are key aspects of influencing. The ability to paint pictures is essential. One can paint a bright or a dark picture of the future, or even both in order to clearly convey the implications and consequences of a course of action.

As Richard Olivier says, 'Henry throughout the play demonstrates the wonderful leadership quality of painting pictures of the future'. Shakespeare is clearly aware of this and uses very strong images, symbols and metaphors. He uses adjectives in a very original and emphatic way to help conjure up the visual images – the *blind and bloody* soldier, the *naked* infants, the *shrill, shrieking* daughters and so on.

One of the most famous influential speeches in the English language is King Henry's speech to his army on the eve of the battle of Agincourt. In this speech King Henry's cousin Duke of Westmoreland laments the fact that they are so few, and wishes that they were more:

> *O that we now had here*
> *But one ten thousand of those men in England*
> *That do no work today!*

But Henry chastises him – rather than agreeing that they need more men, which would only serve to demotivate them, he says that they don't need or want any more. Those that are there are the privileged few – the glory will be theirs alone! So he is able to influence them away from lamenting the small numbers to being glad that they are – *we few, we happy few!*

The real Henry V was one of the first leaders to realise the importance of good communication and used to send regular letters back to England where they would be read out loud throughout the shires. So he would influence remotely even at that period.

We are not suggesting, of course, that you would ever have to deliver threats and the bloodthirsty type of appeals that we have seen above. What we do suggest though, is that you take inspiration from Shakespeare and other writers, their creative use of language and images, their graphic use of language, and make your language creative, exciting and impactful! What pictures of the future do you paint? Do you use eloquent and creative language? Or do you just content yourself to enumerate facts and figures?

Watch videos/dvds of famous speeches and pay attention also to actors' use of body language, intonation and rythmn. In a sense we are all actors when we influence – better to be a good one than a poor one!

Storytelling

Rolf Jensen is a Dane and former CEO of the Copenhagen Institute for Futures Studies, described as one of the largest future oriented think tanks in the world. Jensen has moved on to found the Dream Company and describes himself as Chief Imagination Officer. Jensen tells us that the future lies in what he calls the Dream Society, that we have moved on from the Information society to the Dream society as we have moved on from the Agricultural society through the Industrial society and on through the Information/knowledge society to the Dream Society. The essence of the Dream society is storytelling and experience.

To illustrate he tells us the story of the egg in Denmark. Not so long ago an egg was an egg. A cheap staple food – low priced, simple – basically a commodity. When we were kids an egg was an egg was an egg. Now the egg has changed – in Denmark eggs from free range hens account for more than 50 per cent of the market. Consumers pay more for these eggs – these eggs have a story – they want hens to have access to the earth and the sky, not to have to live in small dark cages. We are now talking about the animals' welfare, we imagine the hens in farmyards 'free range' 'organically fed', we hark back to some rustic vision of the ideal farmyard with hens running clucking around the farm yard. The eggs are of the same quality as before – I personally cannot taste the difference but the evidence is that as consumers we now prefer eggs with stories (in the UK, supermarket chain Waitrose only sells free range eggs). They have names like Columbian Black Hawk, Mabel Pearman's Burford Browns, Straw Bedded Eggs, Intelligent Eating TM, Gladys May's Braddock Whites Free Range Duck Eggs and Old Cotswold Legbar fed on a natural vegetarian cereal diet.

Jensen tells us that the century of materialism is waning and that we as consumers buy more and more with our hearts. Sure, we need a watch to tell the time and the toaster to toast, but more than that we need them to say something about who we are. I can buy a perfectly good reliable guaranteed watch for less than £20 – so why would I need a Rolex? Answer: because a Rolex is much more than a watch; it tells a story about who I am, how much I earn and my position in life.

This is why Rolex have an award which is presented to individuals who represent the Rolex story (The Spirit of Entreprise) through their achievements. Many other companies have a story – Virgin, Aga (selling the story of family togetherness), BMW, and Harley Davidson to name but a few. Many of those who don't are looking for one or inventing one. Scotch whisky has an interesting story to tell, and you will see from advertisements that they are not shy of telling you about the purity of the water, the ancient traditions, the local men whose family have been involved for decades in making the whisky. You might be surprised if you visited some of the distilleries. Some of them are traditional, many of them are modern, and the image is sometimes more of a marketing and influencing tool than a reflection of reality.

The stories of banks used to be represented in their buildings – huge neo classical things (implying solidity, reliability, permanence). Now they've sold off these buildings to pubs and restaurants. So how can banks tell a story these days? Certainly not so much in their buildings which tend to be fairly mundane these days. For example, UK bank Lloyds TSB tells a story of giving and generosity. Their Foundation – one of the biggest charitable givers in the UK, donates 1 per cent of pre tax profits to charity. The Hong Kong and Shanghai Banking Corporation tells us a story of international cooperation and understanding. The Cooperative Bank in the UK promotes ethics and fairness.

So what does this have to do with influence?

The first thing is that companies and organisations use this to try and influence you every day. So you'd better understand this process. The second is that if you are not using this to influence, then your competitors certainly are. So what is your company's story?

What is your personal story? What are you selling? And if you tell us that you're not selling anything, think again! Because people are buying and if you're not telling them your story they're sure as hell reading a story when they see you. They might not believe your story but they will invent one for you anyway. As leading marketing thinker and author of *The Power of Relationship Marketing*, Tony Cram says: 'If you do not tell them a story they're making it up for themselves!'

Jensen tells us that the market will become emotionally defined, and that the product itself will become secondary: 'The product will be an appendix the main purpose of which is to embody whatever story is being told.' Jensen admits that this is pushing things to extreme but that this is definitely the way things are going. The implications for you influencing are clear – what stories are you telling about yourself, your department, your product, your service, your company?

No story means no influence.

Think of any company – try to think of their story. How does it relate to you? In what way does it influence you? Let's look at multinational computer company Hewlett Packard. When one of the authors did some consulting work with them, their internal story was the 'The Shed'. This story told us about where the two founders – Bill Hewlett and Dave Packard-used to work late in the evening to invent their products and service. The story is that Dave and his wife moved into the first floor flat of a house at 367 Addison Avenue, in Palo Alto California. Bill rented the shed behind the house, and the two of them worked on developing the products and management style which turned the company into the multi billion dollar giant it is today. It is interesting that HP pasted pictures of the Shed all over their walls from America to Singapore. The aim was perhaps to humanise the company, or to motivate their employees to work hard in the same way that the founding fathers did. In any case the company felt that it was important to tell the story of its beginnings.

Intel makes a product which we never see, know nothing about, but we all know the name! Why? It is because they realise that commodification is the enemy. They needed to differentiate, so they started advertising not Business to Business but Business to the general public. Objective differentiation is difficult in an age where many products are similar. (Can you tell the difference between the objective picture quality of a Sony TV or a Samsung?) So a subjective appeal to hearts and minds becomes key. So Intel promotes reliability and quality with their hook phase, 'Intel Inside'. This is known as Ingredient Marketing, and other examples are Teflon, Lycra, Goretex and Woolmark.

Interestingly Intel are changing both their logo and their slogan. They are doing this in order to broaden their appeal, and move away from their fairly limited technical image, towards one which is more consumer friendly and oriented towards a broader range of products. So the slogan will change from 'Intel Inside', to 'Leap Ahead', and the logo will be modernised.

The Intel brand is considered by Interbrand to be the fifth most valuable in the world. It is worth some 36 billion dollars. Only Coca Cola, Microsoft, IBM and GE are ranked higher.

All these brands have stories and they exert a strong influence on the market.

Take the UK company Everest Double Glazing. Their motto is 'We fit the best!' If you are looking for the cheapest price don't even think of coming to us. But what you will get is (according to their narrative) 'peace of mind'. Unfortunately if the reality does not match the story the result is even worse than having no story!

This is even happening in sport; the Glazer family are buying the story of Manchester United. London Broncos rugby league club this week (July 2005) have tied up a deal with English rugby club Harlequins. They will play at the Harlequins famous ground, The Stoop, wear the famous Harlequins strips, share facilities, merchandising and website. The interesting aspect is that Broncos is an American type of name and it has no connotation or connection to London, in other words, no story! But Harlequins have a story! They are one of the oldest clubs in the country having been founded in 1866. They have one of the most recognisable strips in the game and are recognised for their open style of play. Unfortunately they are currently not playing in England's premier division, having been relegated at the end of the 2004/2005 season. But as we write, they lead their division and are hopeful of promotion.

So now Broncos are Harlequins and have an instant story, which should help them develop sales, loyalty, audiences! We think it is a brilliant idea.

Let's look at some other companies' stories? How about Virgin? What is their story Freedom, difference, underdog, different, trendy, fun loving, musical, sexy, good service ... reinforced by CEO Richard Branson's image: woolly jumpers (his message is I don't need to wear suits), adventurous pursuits (round the world ballooning, ocean crossing records etc). Although the story doesn't stand up so well when the product diversifies too much – Virgin Cola for example, and Virgin trains could put you off flying with the airline! So the story has to be consistent.

The energy company British Petroleum (BP) now describes itself as Beyond Petroleum. Why? It is because it realises the power of telling us a positive story. A counter story – told by Greenpeace for example -could be one of exploitation of the world's reserves, exploitation of people in poor countries, pollution, corruption etc. So BP chooses to tell us a different story – beyond petroleum, investment in natural renewable energy like wind power, solar energy and tidal energy. No matter that this is only a fraction of their business. The message is clear; they want us to see that they are moving beyond petroleum into renewable energy. Their full page advertising in the UK newspapers has colourful drawings of flowers reinforcing this eco-friendly approach. There are competing stories – BP and Greenpeace – for example, and the organisation that tells the best story has the best chance of influencing the public.

Good stories paint a picture of a desired state or future. They use active, positive words. They tell you about the roots of the company or product, its background, where it is coming from. And it uses that as a springboard to the future, where it (or you) can go. A sort of Looking Back to Look Forward.

Cutty Sark Scotch Whisky doesn't tell any stories of drunkenness or hangovers. It promotes responsible drinking and friendship. They also have a story to tell about the origins of the whisky; it goes back to 1923 when one of the partners of wine merchants Berry Bros discussed launching a new whisky. He believed in a new type of whisky which would be light in colour and made only from the finest malt whiskies. The partners had invited a well known Scottish artist James McBey to lunch that day and he suggested the name Cutty Sark and designed the label (this famous ship, a tea clipper, was once the fastest in the world and was built in Scotland). So now the product has a story and a theme. This makes it more distinctive in the market place. Tony Cram once again: 'The essence of a good brand is a good story.'

The message is clear – get yourself a story! The future in influencing customers lies in making a distinction between your product/service and those of the competition. You need to avoid commodification at all costs. One of the key ways of doing this is to tell (or on a more cynical note) invent, a good story. A word of warning though, the reality has to match up to the story. If it doesn't, if the story is just a story with no link to reality, then you are reducing your credibility.

Spiral dynamics

We feel that this relatively new theory has great potential to help explain why it is sometimes so difficult to communicate with another person, and in showing how to adapt our language and actions to others' perspective. It can help us greatly in understanding why it is that we seem to be able to influence and persuade some people rather easily, yet others are totally resistant to our ideas.

Spiral Dynamics is a system created by Don Beck and Chris Cowan based on the work of American psychologist Clare Graves. Graves was a professor of Psychology and he was interested to find out why people think in different ways about just about everything. His theory was that different people are in different stages of psychological development and that this explains why, for example one person believes in world peace, and another in going to war.

The theory is probably still considered fairly eclectic, and there is some divergence between various writers and researchers. However some key thinkers such as American psychologist and philosopher, Ken Wilbur have shown interest in the theory.

The theory

The theory is called Spiral Dynamics because as the spiral (or level) unfolds, it moves to greater complexity. Each turn of the spiral represents a different worldview or set of values. Beck and Cowan call them *memes*. Memes are to our psycho social and organisational DNA what genes are to our biological DNA. Instead of using extravagant names, each of these spirals has a colour code. There are two levels – the first level goes from Beige through to Green, while the second or higher level has Yellow and Turquoise.

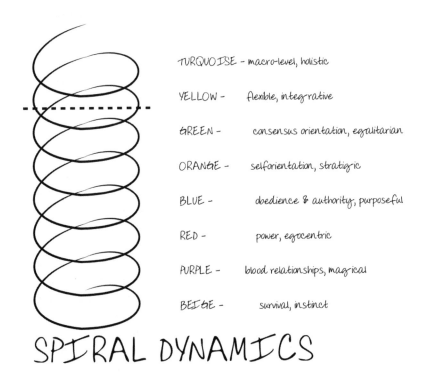

TURQUOISE – macro-level, holistic

YELLOW –   flexible, integrative

GREEN –   consensus orientation, egalitarian

ORANGE –   selforientation, stratigic

BLUE –   obedience & authority, purposeful

RED –   power, egocentric

PURPLE –   blood relationships, magical

BEIGE –   survival, instinct

SPIRAL DYNAMICS

The beige spiral. At the bottom of the spiral you have Beige which represents the basic so-called 'survivalist system'. You see this in babies, the elderly, and in many people in times of great crisis, when there is a temporary regression into this spiral. For example you might say that Beige is the dominant value system in Iraq at the moment, because of the ongoing turbulence there. This level (or meme) is an instinctive, survival based level where you do what you have to do in order to stay alive. People living on the streets would be an example of the Beige level.

Even if you are on a higher level, you might temporarily regress to Beige under extremes of stress or being caught in a crisis situation such as the recent tsunami or the earthquake in Pakistan.

The purple spiral. Next is Purple which speaks of things like 'animistic thinking', a belief in magic, spells etc. People at this stage would form into tribes. There is belief in ancestors who bond the tribe. Kinship and lineage are important. When people believe in voodoo like curses, blood oaths, ancient grudges, rituals and superstitions, then they are acting in the Purple stage. Most of us still have some Purple beliefs. Avoiding walking under ladders, being more careful or not taking a trip on Friday the thirteenth are examples. So too are talismans and the lucky charms we wear.

This stage is seen in some developing countries, gangs, athletic and sports teams, and even in Corporate 'tribes' where there are rituals and tribal customs. Many professional sports teams have rituals and ceremonies which would appear absurd to the outsider. Some New Age beliefs might fall into this level.

The purple company. In organisation terms, you would see nepotism, workers would 'belong' to the paternalistic company which would permeate their lives completely. Tradition would be valued and adhered to without question.

The red spiral. Out of Purple comes Red spiral which describes a strong, ego centric, self centred, selfish level. In this spiral, people, or whole nations would be focussed on Power and what is in it for oneself. This can apply to companies too, so you can see companies at the Red stage of development. Which means that they are fairly unethical and very focussed on money, power and profit. People in this stage see the world as a jungle full of threats and predators, so they think they have to act as conquerors, or outsmart the enemy. It is basically about the law of the jungle where the strongest or most cunning survive. You can see this in teenage rebellion, mercenary soldiers, villains in Hollywood movies, over the top rock stars, bullying managers and unethical businesses.

The red company. In Red organisations you would see the belief that people were naturally lazy and evil and need to be controlled. Those who have very little – the 'have nots' – would be seen to be those who do not deserve much. 'The haves' are entitled to their position and perks. Nobody can be trusted and anybody can be bought.

The blue spiral. After Red comes Blue. The Blue spiral portrays a search for meaning and purpose.In this spiral one would typically conform to rules and regulations, to order. People in this stage would tend to sacrifice the now in order to achieve something at a later date. People would believe in an all powerful Order or Other. There is an absolute belief in what is right and what is wrong, and violating the code has severe penalties and repercussions. By contrast, following the code leads to rewards, either in this life or in an afterlife. In the Blue spiral there are rigid social hierarchies, paternalistic thinking, and one way of doing and thinking. Examples are Puritan America, The Bible belt, Confucian China, Maoist China, Islamic Fundamentalism, Patriotism, the 'Moral majority' and authoritarian structures. It is a purposeful and authoritarian level.

The blue company. In organisation terms a Blue company would be one where employees need to be shown what to do, they would be punished for failure (and rewarded for success) Workers are seen as cogs in the machine and should be loyal to the company because it provides them with jobs and security.

The orange spiral. Then comes the Orange spiral. This describes a more autonomous level where people are less prepared to accept rules and more willing to try and change things. This level is about individual freedom and autonomy and independence. The focus here is on self as opposed to the collective and is said to be the dominant value system in the world today. The world is seen as a rational machine with natural laws that can be learned, mastered and used for one's own purposes. The focus is on achievement and materialistic gains and can be seen in Wall Street materialism, consumerism, large corporations, fashion industry, liberal self interest, Economic Liberalism etc. This is the level of the marketplace, where opportunities and possibilities abound.

The orange company. In Orange organisations there is a belief that workers do want to get ahead and they have much more say and influence than in Blue companies. The belief is that people are motivated by money and want to acquire material rewards. Competition is seen as good, even within the organisation, as it fosters growth and productivity.

The green spiral. Moving on from Orange there is the Green spiral. This spiral represents a shift away from 'I/me/mine' thinking towards 'we/us/our'. The focus is less selfish and more humanistic. There is a focus on ecology, community, networking, and movement away from greed, dogma and divisiveness. There is an emphasis on dialogue, relationships and consensus. It is more egalitarian, anti -hierarchical, has pluralistic values, values diversity and multiculturalism.

But that can only happen at a certain level of development – that is when all the basic needs of food, security etc. have been met. So you don't get green in Afghanistan at the moment (although there will be individuals at that level there).

The green company. In the Green organisation this perspective leads to having more social concerns, having a more ethical perspective on doing business. This might result in an organisation having a greater focus on social responsibility as well as on making profits. You would expect that employees would be less competitive and want to get along well with their colleagues. The belief is that sharing will lead to better results than competition. Emotions are taken into account as much as facts and logic. Everybody in the organisation is an asset and everybody is entitled to contribute and be listened to, and taken seriously. There is a belief that the organisation should look after its community and be socially responsible.

The Green spiral can be seen in Ecology movements, postmodernism, humanistic psychology, animal rights movements, feminism, World Council of Churches, Counselling and Therapy, Gaia movement etc. In business this would manifest itself in a more egalitarian approach underpinned by consensual processes.

All these spirals represent what Graves and Beck call first tier systems. After the first tier there is the second tier. The first level in the second tier is Yellow which is the cutting edge level of development in today's world.

The yellow spiral. In the Yellow stage of development, you can look back at the other stages and see where there are serious problems. People at the Yellow level are equipped to help others at the lower levels, and would be less selfish, and more altruistic than people in the first tier.

The yellow company. A Yellow organisation would be one where people enjoy their work and find meaning in it. Motivation would come not from profit or fear but through learning and understanding. All the information would be available to all employees. Employees would naturally take the role that suits them best rather than being defined by the role. An example of such a company might be Ricardo Semler's Semco company in Brazil. In this company employees are free to look at the books, get all the financial information, and choose who they want to work with etc.

The turquoise level. Turquoise speaks of a more spiritual level and allegedly not many people have attained this level.

The turquoise company. This model states that if there were an organisation at this level it would be one where there was a strong belief in spiritual bonds, where all the organisation was fully responsible for all its activities and impact on the planet.

Graves points out that these are not types of people but systems in people, so you may be green but sometimes you can regress to beige or green or orange. It's the same for companies.

Do you recognise any of the above – either in terms of people, organisations or cultures?

Clearly it is unlikely that a company or a person would have a pure colour. It is likely to be mixed, say Orange-green, for example. And even then other levels would take precedence according to the situation and context. But the overall shape should be fairly recognisable.

So where is your company, your organisation, your boss? What is your level?

So what has this to do with influencing?

The basic link to Influencing is that if you want to influence a person who is at the Red stage then you have to use Red values and Red language. If for example some one is racist and thinks that a person from a particular race or with a different colour of skin is inferior to them, then no amount of logical tolerant Green type of argument will work. If someone is scared and afraid because they feel threatened and are caught, even temporarily, in Beige, then you can only communicate effectively with them by using Beige values and Beige language.

Similarly if a person or a company is Orange – self focussed and self centred in outlook, you will need to talk to them using an Orange frame if you are to have any influence. If someone wants more money and a car and holiday abroad, no amount of talk about sharing, about starving people in Ethopia for example, the dangers of climate warming, the amount of water wasted in swimming pools and golf courses in dry countries will have any impact!

If you want to influence them effectively you will have to frame your arguments based on their level or spiral.

According to Beck and Cowan organisations have *memes* which will determine their basic culture. The people in the organisation also have dominant memes which shape their life values and priorities.

You need therefore to be aware of the spiral on which the culture, organisation or person is operating on, and bear that in mind when developing your influencing case. If an employee is short of money and worried about job security then you might place him or her in this context in the Beige spiral. To communicate effectively with this person and to have a chance of being influential you would need to address these issues in terms of what they related to. He/she is concerned with survival and no amount of talk around profitability, shareholders, growth and market share will have any effect. You would have to settle the survival or fear factor first before you could move on to the issues which concern you as a manager, which might well be Red if your organisation is focused on profitability and shareholder value.

You can see how companies already use these spirals. The workforce of a company where redundancies are about to be announced will respond in typical Beige fashion. Sales managers use contests incentives and competitions to raise Orange values. In an organisation whose culture is Green, then there will be meetings where feelings are shared, systems which allow expression of challenge, and it will be permissible to express emotions.

If, as consultants based in an academic environment, we feel disposed towards the Green spiral and talk about Emotional Intelligence, participation, and the necessity to allow challenge in an organisation, we can face scepticism from hard bitten managers who see their job as pushing their people to achieve even higher targets. They will not accept that achievement can be gained by participative methods. They might accuse us of being 'touchy feely', or 'out of touch'.

EXAMPLE

Interestingly, some rich people in China have taken to skiing in indoor skiing centres in Beijing. The amount of water they use is enormous, as is the power necessary to refrigerate the snow and keep the environment at a low enough temperature. Although Beijing has both problems with power and water and the Government is unlikely to allow any more of these ski centres to open, the people who use them focus on their own pleasure, how hard they have worked etc. and not on the effect it has on their fellow citizens. So here is a situation where there is a very clear need to conserve power and water, yet the people who are the wealthiest in that society are wasting much needed resources. But trying to influence them not to ski on the basis of the wasted resources is ineffective.

Their main focus of interest doesn't seem to lie in what happens to this group of 'others', as it would seem that they would rely on having the wealth to ensure their own supplies. They are at the Orange level. To influence them effectively would necessitate using Orange language and actions. So the local government can forbid the building of such centres, or fine, tax and/or penalise the builders and operators. With regard to users they would need to demonstrate clearly that continued use of such centres would result in them having no energy, air conditioning or water. That might be difficult as the users by definition have more access to resources than the average Beijing citizen. The use of hierarchical or official power and sanctions might be the most effective, if not the only, way to persuade users to stop.

Exercise

Think about where you might be in terms of Spiral Dynamics. How do you normally react? What range of colours do you use? What about your family, friends, colleagues, and clients?

How self aware are you? How flexible are you? Think back to situations where you did not influence effectively; could it be that you were framing the situation from a spiral perspective that is different from the other people involved? What could you have done to frame the situation differently?

Can you notice the language of others? Might they be reacting to a situation for example in Red, but you talk to them from the Green perspective? If that were the case they would be less likely to be influenced by you than if you were able to respond – initially at least – on their own terms and perspective.

✍ SUMMARY OF KEY POINTS

We have reviewed a variety of different approaches and techniques all of which can be useful to add to your influencing toolbox. Use of these various techniques obviously depends upon the situations and the various people involved. The tools we have covered are:

- ☛ Link and build
- ☛ Framing and reframing
- ☛ Ask and listen
- ☛ Shared rewards
- ☛ Language of influence
- ☛ Create a compelling case
- ☛ Relate emotionally
- ☛ Just Do It!
- ☛ The influencing staircase
- ☛ Influencing in Shakespeare
- ☛ Storytelling
- ☛ Spiral Dynamics

7 Deciding on and Implementing Your Influencing Strategy

Putting It into Practice

> *So, which direction should we all travel? Whose agenda is it?*
> *I suppose the best scenario is that it is my direction and our*
> *agenda, everyone wanting the same, a win-win*
>
> Nigel Melville. Former Director of Rugby at
> Wasps and Gloucester

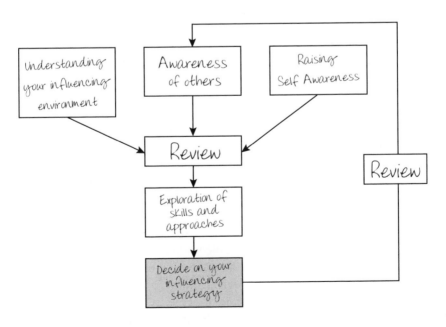

A MODEL FOR INFLUENCING

We have now reached the stage when it is important to focus on how you plan to approach all the various people you need to influence in order to get buy in to your ideas. There are a wide variety of approaches that we all use on a day to day basis all of which can involve aspects of influencing about your issue. Hopefully by raising your awareness of the variety of influencing approaches and also encouraging you to think about the most appropriate approach for the person and situation this will help you to plan an effective influencing strategy for your influencing issues in the future.

Deciding upon and adopting the appropriate influencing strategy for the particular situation you are involved in is a skill in itself. Influencing strategy is about how you execute your influencing plan, taking account of the environment, the others involved, your own style and the skills, techniques and tools you wish to use.

To highlight what we mean by this we can use a sporting analogy of a football match: the players develop their skills – passing, tackling, dribbling, etc. – but real skill in this area is only effective if they use these skills appropriately and adopt the best strategies for the situation they are facing, for instance knowing when to pass, when to shoot, who to pass to, etc. A similar situation exists while influencing; for instance, knowing yourself, the others and the environment is one element but selecting the right approach, style and skills in any given influencing situation is what makes for a successful outcome. If you choose the wrong ones you can miss your goal completely – just as you can if you adopt the wrong strategy when playing football.

However in addition to selecting the right style, skills, techniques and tactics you also have to consider the variety of different approaches you could use for implementing your influencing strategy, for instance, in a meeting, a presentation or a report.

The choice of approach can be pivotal in achieving your goal. In most complex influencing situations several different approaches are necessary. What works for one person may not work for another so it is often necessary to use a variety of approaches to achieve your overall goal.

For each of these approaches it is always important to consider your environment, your own preferences and styles, the others, your skills and the techniques and tactics to adopt. These aspects of influencing have all been covered in previous chapters. What we wish to explore now is the variety of different approaches available to you as part of your implementation process. It is important to stress here that it will almost always be necessary to use a variety of approaches for any important situation as it is rare that 'influencing is ever a one shot effort'! Influencing is nearly always a process and not an event, so this means that it involves not only awareness of the self, others and the environment but agility and capability in using your skill, techniques and tactics in a variety of settings.

In our experience of working with thousands of participants on our programmes, our day to day working lives and data we have collected in our research, we have identified nine different approaches that people adopt on a regular basis. Each of these approaches bring their own challenges and what follows is an exploration of each approach, highlighting in each case tips for success.

Key approaches

STRATEGY

USE OF INFORMAL NETWORKS

These are the people you interact with on a day to day basis. Making use of these informal networks to sow seeds of interest in your ideas and to test your ideas out can be very beneficial before moving to more formal situations. Your informal networks can help you formulate your ideas and plans. They are more likely to give you honest feedback about the issue and the approach you plan to take. Most of us have several different networks sometimes related to the different parts of a business that we operate in and this in itself can provide you with useful intelligence about those you have to influence. These networks can act as mutual challenge and support mechanisms if developed in the right manner.

The key to success in using your informal networks is to identify who will have an interest/involvement in the issue on which you are influencing; creating a stakeholder map can help with this. Then you should create opportunities for informal interaction and conversation. Informal networks provide you with a wonderful opportunity to gather information, test out your ideas and to add allies to your stakeholder list.

A CORRIDOR CONVERSATION

It is sometimes also known as an elevator pitch. Typically this is an informal conversation where you, the influencer, grab an opportunity when it comes your way. An example of a good corridor conversation opportunity might be:

You meet your boss in the car park in the morning, you haven't seen him/her for a few days and you don't have a scheduled meeting for another two weeks. You have been thinking for some time that you need to get the boss on side about the project you are working on. This is the ideal opportunity, it takes five minutes to walk from the car park to your boss's office so you have to be focussed and get the key points across as quickly as possible to enable you to determine his position on the issue.

Important aspects of a corridor conversation are, firstly to recognise the opportunity for what it is – a chance to chat to someone in an informal way about your influencing issue. This demands that you are sufficiently well versed with and prepared about the issue. And you should be aware of the key stakeholders to take the opportunity when it arises. You could use the chance to either question, advocate, present your ideas or explore broad issues. If the focus of the corridor conversation is about getting your point across to the other party then it is clear that you need to be articulate, concise and structured both in the content and in the process. Corridor conversations are all about taking opportunities when they arise and then making the most of the occasion. So, to make best use of any opportunity that presents itself you should think through what you might say, identify the three to five key points that best give a flavour/overview of your issue and keep in mind who the key people are so that you can take advantage of situations as they arise.

AN EMAIL

In this technological age more and more frequently we rely on Email as one of our main forms of communication. This means that Email is often used as the first stage in an influencing discussion. Some of the key issues in using Email when influencing are in relation to the content and tone of the message. Typically Emails are seen as an informal communication medium where short messages are conveyed between individuals or groups of individuals. In using Email as part of your influencing strategy you must consider the following:

▶ Firstly, recognise that you are using it as part of your influencing approach; the message it contains will convey some meaning to the reader/s and will have some impact upon their response and approach to your issue.
▶ Who the Email should be sent to is important for all sorts of reasons. This can indicate to others how important the issue is, how important they themselves are in relation to the issue, who else will be involved and therefore who they should network with in order to work on the issue and who they can set up allegiances with. Also in relation to this is the issue of how you address the Email, for instance, with lots of addressees on one Email or a single addressee but send the same Email to several people or with cc's and bcc's. All have advantages and dis-advantages.
▶ The information contained in the Email and how to make it appealing to all your recipients including the structure, tone, words, punctuation and level of detail. One of the biggest issues discussed on our training programmes in relation to this whole area is the way that Emails can be 'misread' so easily. We all interpret messages through different lenses and therefore it is very easy without the benefit of immediate two way interaction for someone to pick up the wrong idea from your message. Because of this it might be a good idea to ask others to read the contents prior to sending to ensure it is clearly conveying the mes-sage you intend and that some hidden meaning is not possible. This is particularly important if the Email is going to a large group of people.
▶ It is also useful to remember to give an indication in your Email as to what you expect in return or as a response to your message.

ONE TO ONE DISCUSSION

This is often the approach that people feel most comfortable with. Meeting with one other person to discuss the issue appears to be the least stressful of the approaches used when influencing others. However, like the other approaches there is much room for failure. The major benefit of a one to one discussion is that for the actual interaction you only have to consider your self and the other person involved so planning and prepar-ing should be simple, or is it?

In a one to one discussion you really have to get it right first time with that person or you could set off on the wrong foot immediately and alienate them toward both yourself and your issue. Focussing on the other person and planning for a discussion by putting yourself in their shoes in relation to this issue is the key. Adopting an approach that will capture the other person's attention and interest right from the start will be important. Work should be done prior to the meeting in terms of identifying some or all of the following:

▶ Where the individual stands in relation to your issue – supporter, opposes, winner, loser, neutral, etc ...
▶ What motivates and demotivates the individual
▶ How formal/informal the person is in normal circumstances
▶ Extrovert or introvert
▶ Have they a preference for detail or big picture
▶ What style might appeal to him/her

The issue when influencing in a one to one discussion scenario is to recognise what your goal is and plan and prepare to meet that goal by focussing on the other person, their needs and how best to gain their attention, interest and commitment.

AN INFLUENCING MEETING (OF UP TO ABOUT EIGHT PEOPLE)

Most meetings present people with the opportunity for influencing. Much of course will depend upon the nature of the meeting and will then help to determine how you prepare for it. However, let's assume that this is an important meeting and you know you will at some point have the opportunity to influence the others in attendance about your latest project. At this stage you need their interest and commitment. Let's also make the assumption that you know all the people attending the meeting.

If this is the case then you have no excuse whatsoever for lack of preparation. This preparation should include doing a stakeholder map to identify what you know about each person involved and to help you make the best possible plans and choices when influencing them. This can also assist you in planning your own behaviour, style and approach. The things you may wish to consider include:

▶ What is your role in the meeting?
  ▷ Did you call it?
  ▷ Are you chairing it?
  ▷ Are you simply an invitee?

We find that the role you play in the meeting will have a major impact on the process of the meeting. For instance, if you called the meeting you are likely to have more influence about the attendees, venue, timing and agenda, thus giving you significantly more control over the process.

► What are your power bases? Understanding your power position can help you to understand the behaviour of others. Are you the boss and therefore more likely to have the final say anyway, or have more information, or more clout. Are you an expert in the area and therefore already have a track record of success and a high level of credibility? Do you hold the purse strings and thus the resources in relation to this issue? As we have already seen in Chapter 5 power in any given situation can be attributed to various aspects of personality, position, knowledge, experience or relationships; the important thing is to be aware of it and how best to use it, and *not* to misuse it!

► Should you plan for a formal or more informal intervention? Planning is important whether you are attending a formal or informal meeting; and as the novelist, Mark Twain (1835–1910) said 'it usually takes more than 3 weeks to prepare a good impromptu speech'. Formal meetings probably have pre set agendas, papers in advance, a chairperson and minutes. Less formal meetings may also have all these features but then again they may not. The issue here is to think about what's appropriate for the type of meeting: in a formal meeting it is probably best to opt for the more formal approach possibly a written report followed by a presentation; in an informal meeting you probably have more choice in the approaches used. The approaches that you do select should be in relation to the issue, the people involved, your style and skills.

► Is it appropriate to plan a formal presentation where you set out your case in a very upfront way? Clearly if this is the case then it is important to ensure you pave the way and do your preparation and planning. In particular make the organiser aware of your intention. (More about presentations later)

► Might a more informal sharing of ideas and asking questions be more appropriate? For this approach it is important to be clear about how far you will go in sharing your ideas and the questions you might ask to elicit information and views from your colleagues. Know what you want from others and how much you are willing to share with others.

► Should you give prior warning by circulating a written paper or Email with your initial thoughts? Sometimes giving people prior warning of an issue can lead to a richer discussion; however, it can also lead to more challenge or even more support.

► At what stage in the proceedings would it be best to bring up your issue and will you have any control over this anyway? At some meetings timing is in our own hands; at others it will be made for you. The important issue is to be prepared for any eventuality.

▶ How well do you know all the attendees, and how sure are you that you can anticipate their behaviour in relation to your influencing issue? Knowing your stakeholders and their position regarding your influencing issue can help you enormously in planning your behaviour, the content and process for the meeting. Again your stakeholder map can help here. Anticipating people's behaviour and planning how you might deal with it will be time well spent. In terms of the attendees, knowing their typical behaviour in meetings will help; for instance, do they usually question for detailed knowledge and understanding, will they be happy to hear the big picture and go with that, will they offer suggestions in relation to the issue, are they the sort of person who challenges no matter what the issue is? Having a general picture in your mind of each person's usual behaviour pattern can give you an advantage.

▶ Where is the meeting taking place? Is it on your home territory in your own office, somebody else's office or in a meeting room? In all of these cases at least you should be aware of the venue and have some control over layout of the room. If the meeting is offsite at another office, in a hotel or conference centre then you will have less control. The relevant issue here is who is organising the meeting, if you are in charge of this remember to take control and ensure you have all the necessary equipment and comforts for your needs.

▶ What will be the room layout? Seems like a simple thing but layout is important in any meeting situation, and even more so when influencing. Obviously much depends upon the number of people attending, and some of the important things to consider are:

  ▷ Being able to see and establish eye contact with as many of the attendees as possible
  ▷ Ensuring that you can clearly see and maintain eye contact with the main decision makers
  ▷ You can afford to have your supporters slightly outside your eye contact probably by your side; however those you know will challenge you should be easy to see.
  ▷ A round table is best for meetings of up to about eight people; if this is not possible then arrange as square a set up as you can manage with the tables available.

Where you sit in relation to the others and having the ability to observe their body language and facial expression can be extremely useful in meetings. Watching out for signs of support can be confidence boosting, observing other cues and clues, for instance noticing that someone appears puzzled can signal it's time to stop and clarify, test understanding, summarise or allow questions. Observing postures, gestures, facial expressions and levels of eye contact are all ways of assessing how well your ideas are going down with the attendees.

THE INFLUENTIAL PRESENTATION

Most presentations involve an element of influencing so the following guidelines can be applied in most situations that demand a presentation. But, when you are actually setting out to be influential in your presentation and your aim is to influence your audience to buy into your idea and commit to action then it is important to consider how you can make your presentation memorable and appropriate for the topic and audience. Presentations are more than simply beginnings, middles and endings; they are a performance where you are taking your audience's time to listen to you. It is therefore critical for you to make good use of this time and to ensure that you give yourself the best possible opportunity to influence effectively.

With this in mind the following model summarises the key areas to consider when putting together an influential presentation. Before we examine the key elements it is important to agree what an influential presentation involves. An influential presentation is one where the presenters demonstrate a confident, clear and articulate presentation of their issue, the aim of which is to gain the attention and interest of the audience in such a way that they want to:

▶ buy in to your ideas
▶ explore your ideas further with them
▶ Commit to action

When creating an influential presentation one has to pay attention to both the content and process as the model below illustrates. We would encourage planning and preparation in both areas.

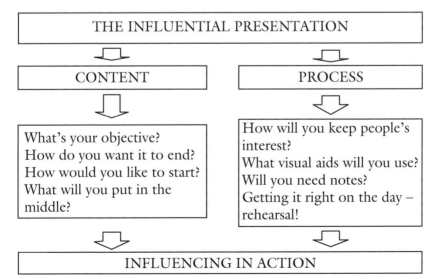

Let's focus first on the content and the four areas, namely the objective, the ending, the start and the middle.

CONTENT

▶ **What's your objective?** Developing a short, clear and focussed objective and keeping this uppermost in your mind throughout the preparation, planning and presentation phases should contribute to a successful presentation. It is best to capture your objective in a short phrase, sentence or paragraph. For instance: 'My objective is to share thoughts about the new performance management system and gauge initial reactions' or 'My objective is to persuade the audience to buy a new computer system for client relationship management' One way of helping you to create your objective is to ask yourself what you want your audience to say, do, ask or believe when they have finished listening to you. This is all about putting yourself in the audiences' shoes and asking yourself what's in it for them. You should write down your objective and keep it visible to you during your preparatory and planning phase. This helps you to focus when making decisions about the content.

In the instance of an influential presentation the main purposes will almost certainly be to persuade your audience of something, and in addition to influencing them you also have to impart information, enthuse and interest them.

▶ **How do you want to end your presentation?** It may seem a little bizarre to focus on the ending before examining any other aspect of the content. However, as the final words you say in any presentation are the memories your audience will leave with, getting this right involves planning both the words and the approach you wish to take. Remember you only have one chance to leave a lasting impression and influential message. The last message should be memorable and should convey the essence of your presentation, any action you wish taken and any decisions you require. It is important to think about it, plan it out and focus on how you can best get your final points across.

People remember best what they hear last so it is worth rehearsing it and memorising it to get it right. Most of us end presentations by taking questions, and sometimes this can work incredibly well especially if you have a high level of agreement to your ideas; however, sometimes it can go very wrong. For instance, let's say you are presenting about a highly emotive subject and you know that your audience will have mixed views. At best you would hope for a proportion of the audience to buy in and support you with others lukewarm but willing to listen and others in complete opposition. In this case you may expect some tricky questions. If these questions or comments detract from your message then this is what the audience may remember rather than your final positive closing statements. Bearing this in mind it can be beneficial to take questions just before you make your final closing statement. How does this work? After you have finished the main thrust of your presentation, pause and tell the audience 'Before I make my final closing remarks perhaps we can have a short question time'; then take questions for the appropriate time; then thank them and go into your final statement. In this way you grab their attention again and have the opportunity to finish with your own strong, positive comments rather than people hearing the answer to the last question.

Interesting endings include:

▷ Asking for action – what, when and how
▷ Summary of content – short and simple – 3 key points is enough
▷ A quote which sums up your talk
▷ A picture, image or cartoon that sums up your talk
▷ A relevant metaphor or story – again that sums up the key points

► **How would you like to start off?** The beginning of any presentation provides you with a real opportunity to create an impression, grab attention and to encourage people to listen with interest. However, as we have already seen in previous chapters you only have a few minutes to make a first impression. As this is the case it is almost certainly worth practising and memorising your opening minutes and it means not just the words but also the approach. In addition to this there are two prerequisites which are important for all presentations and should always be attended to. These are to start on time and ensure your audience know who you are and what gives you the right to speak on the subject. In relation to your introduction the timing of this should be appropriate to the remainder of your introduction. So, for instance you may choose to cover certain introductory statements relating to the content of your presentation prior to your own personal introduction.

Other factors to take into account when planning the beginning of your presentation are:

▷ Ask yourself what's in it for your audience, put yourself in their shoes and ask yourself why they should listen to you
▷ To clearly state the purpose and your perspective on the topic
▷ How you will capture their attention and interest

Interesting openings include:
▷ State your objective right at the start – don't keep it a secret
▷ A quote, famous saying which leads into your talk
▷ Showing an example of whatever you are talking about; for instance, if you are talking about a product show that product.

▷ Start with a personalised story that is relevant to the topic
▷ Attention getting and appropriate video/dvd footage

▶ **What will you put in the middle?** If you have achieved your aim in your introduction then you should have an audience who are primed to listen to further information about your topic. Your job now is to give the audience sufficient information to understand the issue and to persuade them about it. There are many different approaches for effectively presenting a persuasive case and most of these include stating the facts and your evidence followed by your reasons for your case.

Some of the most common approaches for the middle part of any presentation include:

▷ Stating the advantages and disadvantages of your ideas
▷ Defining the problem and offering suggested solutions
▷ Focussing on the past or the old ways of doing things then proposing possible solutions or new ideas
▷ Itemising the features and benefits
▷ Talk about your ideal outcome then the reality

It is in this middle bit that people can go dramatically wrong by being:

▷ Too detailed
▷ Not detailed enough
▷ Taking too long or
▷ Too short

Turning people off during the middle of any presentation can have a hugely negative effect upon the influencing content. This is why it is so important to consider both content and process when putting it together.

Now let's look at the process element of the presentation.

PROCESS

▶ **How will you keep people's interest?** Keeping people's interest throughout is one of the biggest challenges for any presenter or speechmaker. Different people have different spans of attention and often their span of attention will vary in relation to the subject of the discussion. If it is something that really turns them on then they are more likely to pay more attention but even then there will be times when people drift off. However if the subject is something that doesn't grab your attention then the likelihood of listening fully and attentively throughout is limited. So what can you do to get and keep people's attention?

Putting yourself in the audience's shoes always helps. By understanding why they might be sitting there you can tailor what you are saying to them personally or to them as a group.

Body language can be another way to add interest; think of ways to make yourself interesting to look at: what you wear, what you do with your hands and arms, do you walk around or stand still, and what is your facial expression saying to the audience. Eye contact with different members of the audience as well as scanning the whole audience frequently together with the appropriate facial expression can encourage people to listen.

▷ Paralanguage varying your pitch, pace, timing, tone and pause level and making your voice interesting to listen to.
▷ Posing questions to the audience, possibly using people's names to invite their comment. But be careful with this one; if you get it wrong some people can feel put on the spot and thus defensive by this behaviour. Pre-warning people can help.
▷ Asking for questions at various different stages throughout can be interesting but can also knock out your timing.
▷ If you are using lots of data in your presentation then think about the best format for illustrating it. For instance, rather than simply using a table of numbers a graph, a histogram or a pie chart might demonstrate your point more effectively.
▷ Use visual aids (see next section).
▷ Use of quotes, mnemonics and thought provoking statements can all add impact and interest.
▷ Telling stories and anecdotes can personalise and bring a talk to life, making it more interesting for the listener.

> I try to use examples which people can relate to rather than simply theory, rhetoric and anecdote

Participant, Ashridge Influencing
Strategies and Skills Programme

Above all energy and enthusiasm are the key to success; demonstrating your enthusiasm for your topic and speaking with energy and passion can lead to use of many of the above techniques.

Here's an example of a really interesting presentation we heard several years ago when we were running a short course.

EXAMPLE

The situation: The participants had been briefed to prepare a short presentation on a topic of their own choice to inform us about something they were enthusiastic/passionate about.

The presentation: The topic was 'The Classic Malts': it was about the six types of classic malt whisky that the United Distillers Company was marketing at that time. The presenter had only one prop (or so we thought) and that was a map of Scotland. He was the last presenter of the evening (we'd already listened to five others) and what happened in the next 20 minutes or so was an informative, entertaining and memorable talk.

He introduced his topic and then began to talk about each of the six classic malts in turn really making the whisky come to life, describing the area of Scotland that it came from and therefore what gave it its flavour, for instance the peatiness, the heather's scent, purity of the local water, the quality of the barley etc., talking about the whisky in very much the same way as a wine taster would describe a fine wine. Then he produced from his jacket a miniature bottle of the whisky. Each description was short, visual, colourful and actually made one's mouth salivate in anticipation of the actual taste. What he'd done was capture several of our senses in his descriptions, sight, hearing, taste, and then his stroke of genius came at the end when he invited us all to taste the one that appealed to us the most.

Quite brilliant and certainly one of the most memorable presentations we have heard in many years of running presentation skills programmes. It certainly influenced us to be more aware of the benefits of a good malt over a blended whisky!

▶ **What visual aids will you use?** Power point, flipchart, video clip, dvd clip, still picture, the real thing! Many presenters use their visual aids as their own memory joggers and forget that they can be mighty powerful as attention getters and keepers but can also act as a complete turn off. No doubt many of you will have been at presentations (influential or not) where you have experienced what we call 'death by power point'! Power point is so easy to get wrong; however if you adhere to the following few simple rules you shouldn't go too far wrong:

  ▷ Keep them short and simple (KISS)
  ▷ Use pictures (must be relevant) and words
  ▷ Translate numbers into charts
  ▷ Make sure all words and figures are big enough to be readable by the audience

▷ Maximum six lines of text per slide

▷ Use colour but not too much

▷ Avoid complex animations; animations are good when used appropriately

▷ Be comfortable and confident in using the medium you choose. Many a presenter has fallen foul of the 'technical glitch'; something not going quite right at the outset that upsets your confidence and delivery throughout.

The main thing to remember about visual aids is that they must be visual and an aid, an aid for your audience not for you.

▶ **Will you need notes?** We all need notes or memory joggers especially when undertaking what for many of us is quite a challenging and demanding experience. Notes act as a prop during the presentation, often giving us confidence rather than anything else. One should not feel ashamed of using them; even the best presenters refer to notes. Auto cue is one of the more advanced approaches and this is used all the time by presenters on television and at conferences. If you have to use auto cue as your note system then it is important to practise, as it takes real skill to read and yet appear natural and chatty at the same time. Try watching political conferences or awards ceremonies and observe the presenters you will soon be able to sort the skilful presenters from the less skilful. Some of you may remember the disastrous Brit Award ceremony several years ago where Mick Fleetwood and Samantha Fox were the main presenters and were clearly not very skilled with auto cue. They appeared wooden, got the timing all wrong and often spoke each other's words.

Power point slides have a place for writing your cue notes on one of the screens; this is an excellent system and enables you to print off a copy of your slide with the notes relating to that slide. This is very useful both before and during the presentation. Reading your notes just prior to the presentation helps you to remember the general gist of the content then during the presentation you can have your notes handy for use just in case you need them.

Another popular note system is to put key word notes onto cue cards, small cards of about 3 inches × 4inches. Onto these cards you should put key words as reminders for you while you are talking. It is important that you put only a few words onto each card and use writing that is easy and clear to read. Stapling the cards together is also a good idea just in case you get them out of order or drop them!

▶ **Getting it right on the day – rehearsal!** There are many ways of rehearsing and many benefits to be gained. We often find that simply talking our presentation plans through with a colleague can be rehearsal enough. Colleagues can give you feedback on the content, approach and suggest ideas for improvements. In particular this can be a useful approach for rehearsing and getting feedback on the important opening and closing statements.

Audio taping or video taping yourself and then reviewing it either yourself or with trusted others can be a great way of rehearsing your talk. In particular this can be helpful for reviewing and understanding your body language and paralanguage. Other ways of running through your presentation are simply to speak it out loud to yourself when you find you have a spare moment, while driving, or in the bath!

A WRITTEN REPORT

It is often a major element of any influencing discussion. Putting our ideas into writing and getting the key points over in an appealing and informative way can be quite a challenge. However, it must not be forgotten that any written report will act as part of the persuasive process just as much as those words uttered orally. The challenges in writing an influential report are related to:

▶ Structure – ensuring that it is clear, logical and flowing. What any reader wants is to be able to read with ease and easily identify the flow of the written document. So choosing the right structure for the topic will be vital.
▶ Content, length and level of detail – how you will get your message across in the words you use, how much detail, what should go into the report and what should be left out. Thinking about your readers and the questions they might ask can be helpful here. Getting the right length of report for the topic and level of detail are also important.
▶ Layout and attractiveness – never underestimate the importance of this element of any written work. The use of bold letters, highlight, paragraphing, charts, pictures and tables all help the reader to follow your content and to buy into your ideas.
▶ Style and audience appeal – as in a verbal interaction, you must select the appropriate style for the intended reader/s. Naturally if your report is targeted at several people then you have to consider them and reflect upon the most appropriate way of having multiple appeals. In general using a combination of push and pull styles in the report should cover it for most people. Often the detail can be covered in any Appendices which appeals to those who wish to have a load of detail and allows those who prefer to see only the big picture to get the general gist in the body of the report.

► Is there a company style you have to follow? If so, follow it and also individualise it with your own brand.

A TELEPHONE CONVERSATION

Again one should never underestimate the importance of a telephone conversation in the influencing process. If during a telephone conversation you touch on your issue then you are beginning to influence about it. As the telephone involves a two way process at least you have the opportunity to question, clarify, test understanding and summarise. However, the bit that's missing is the body language so on the telephone you are completely dependent upon your vocal usage, the actual words and the paralanguage you use to get your message across. The words and paralanguage are going to assume even greater importance, so you need to consider the impact of your voice, accent, intonation, pace, rhythm to ensure that you are not only understood but also influential. The choice of words when using this medium is also important as together these words and the way you say them are the essence of your message. Like all other strategies you can make notes and rehearse and of course smile.

VIDEO CONFERENCE

Organisation and process are the keys with a video conference. It is important to adopt an organised approach to this sort of meeting. Although you have the opportunity to see each other as well as to hear each other it is still a discussion aided by technology and is not like everyone being in the same room at the same time. So some tips are:

► Ask everyone to introduce themselves at the beginning
► Establish some ground rules regarding the process, for instance only one person talking at a time, no interrupting, regular summaries of progress, agree the timings
► Agree on an agenda in advance so that people can be prepared
► Summarise frequently, test understanding and check for divergent views
► Enable differing views to be discussed and aired by using both advocacy and inquiry
► End by summarising what has been agreed, what the next steps are and who is responsible for what
► Thank everyone for their involvement.

EXAMPLE

Remember the stakeholder map back in Chapter 5 where we used the example of the redevelopment and relaunch of an Ashridge development programme. A quick reminder of what the map looked like:

A STAKEHOLDER MAP

This situation involved multiple stakeholders and was reasonably complex as it was a major issue within Ashridge at the time involving making a decision about a programme which had in some form or the other been in our portfolio for over 30 years.

The challenge was actually in two stages, first to convince my boss and the Dean of the college that is was worth investing time and energy in relaunching this programme. In addition to these two people the other key stakeholders at this stage were clients and participants. To ascertain their views I held a couple of *focus group meetings* with past participants and *interviewed* current and past clients. During this process I had *regular meetings* with both my boss and the Dean, keeping them up to date about the progress I was making. These *meetings* were usually *pretty informal* yet I still believe to this day that keeping them both closely involved and informed about the process helped in gaining their commitment and support through out the bigger process.

Having convinced them it was worth the time and effort to now redevelop and relaunch the whole programme the real complexity and hard work began. I began *to analyse my stakeholder map and identified that the key people* now to get on board were the tutor team and the administrators. I used a combination *of informal networking* and *one to one discussion* to gain their support and ideas then invited representatives of all groups to attend a *planning meeting*; invitations were sent by *Email*.

I planned the meeting meticulously as I knew some of the participants were still unsure and unconvinced about certain elements of the current plan. During the meeting I used a combination of a *brief presentation* of initial ideas, together with an *informal brainstorming and idea generation process* to gather new ideas.

In terms of style adopted it was a combination of *visionary, persuasive reasoning and collaboration*. I needed buy in and commitment as this programme involved many of the stakeholders' time and effort to ensure success when we relaunched. Following this meeting we agreed on a main project team who would do most of the design and relaunch work and four months later we relaunched a successful programme, renamed 'Developing Business and Leadership Skills' and shortened from 3 weeks to 12 days!

So, as you can see this whole process involved a range of different approaches, skills, styles and techniques and involved to varying degrees tenacity, energy, enthusiasm, commitment and compromise and while it didn't all go smoothly we got there in the end. The programme continues to run to this day, though it has continued to be subject to constant redevelopment and redesign to maintain its contemporary approach and content.

EXERCISE

► You might find it useful to reflect upon a recent successful influencing scenario that you have dealt with and reflect upon the various stages you went through to achieve success.
► Now focus on a current influencing issue and sketch out your implementation plan.

✍ SUMMARY OF KEY POINTS

Getting it right in terms of putting things into practice is a non scientific process and can even be a bit of a hit and miss affair. Much is down to planning, preparation and analysis. Accepting that influencing is a process not an event, and therefore adopting a variety of approaches and strategies to suit the different environments, situations and characters is key to your success.

Typically any implementation process will involve some or all of the following approaches:

- Using your informal networks
- Taking advantage and creating opportunities for corridor conversations
- Composing and sending Emails
- One to one discussions
- Organising and taking part in both formal and informal meetings
- Planning and making a presentation
- Writing reports
- Telephone conversations
- Taking part in video conferences

8 Conclusion

Tips, Techniques and Misconceptions!

As we have seen from the previous chapters effective influencing is a complex and challenging process. There are no right and wrong ways; there are no magic answers; however there are certain overriding principles which if adhered to will undoubtedly assist you in achieving a successful influencing outcome.

Three key lessons

From our experience in both our own influencing and in teaching the skills of influencing we have identified three key lessons that if respected will result in you being a more effective influencer.

> **Build your credibility**
> **Demonstrate integrity**
> **Develop relationships**

BUILD YOUR CREDIBILITY

If you are not credible, then by definition no one will believe you and if they don't believe you, you won't be very effective at convincing others! But it's amazing how rarely we try to perceive how credible we are in specific circumstances with a specific audience.

We often tend to have what we call the railroad approach, that is we have our own particular way of doing something and we are jolly well going to stick to it (after all if I changed what I did I could be accused of being manipulative couldn't I?) And this is after all the way I am, the real me!

Well sorry, but the real you might be the one that gets you into trouble and who is the real me anyway? An inflexible moron convinced of his own rightness? Or someone prepared to be flexible and alter his style to get better results? You choose.

So how do you build credibility? The first step is to recognise when you are not likely to be credible. The fact is you are not always credible and you will either have to choose not to fight a particular battle (i.e. not try to influence) or build up some credibility in the subject or with the people you want to influence. You can do this through working on the relational aspect or by researching a subject.

But before you rush off to build your credibility, you may need first to consider *unbuilding* your *lack* of credibility! Imagine a credibility scale of 1 to 10 where 10 is world expert and 1 is utter lack of knowledge. If you think you are rated on 1 to 3 then you have a deficit of credibility to face before you can even start to build credibility. It takes time and effort to deconstruct lack of credibility and you need to establish first of all a neutral position before taking an active influencing position. If your reputation with a group or area is poor then you cannot just rush in and hope to positively influence. For example, if you are an engineer hoping to become a coach or leadership specialist then you need to get rid of any negative perceptions by others about you before you can start to actively focus on building a reputation. This might consist of studying for a degree in the area or taking a series of short courses and making sure your colleagues know you are doing this.

If not, then your colleagues who have trained in this area for years may well not recognise your ability (even if you are excellent). Of course an external group of people may have no problem here and recognise your abilities immediately. But in your internal colleagues' eyes you will have little credibility until you do.

The result of being credible is that you have more influencing power. High credibility leads to positive expectations. As an example I once went to study for a diploma in Export marketing at a higher education establishment in England. I enjoyed the studies and had a good relationship with my colleagues and the teaching staff. I noticed quite early on that the lecturers paid attention to my contributions (much more than I had noticed at University!) and even when I said something palpably off the mark they were willing to listen and take it seriously. Intrigued by this unusual (for me) attitude I explored this one evening over a few pints. It turned out that as part of the selection process all candidates had to fill in a questionnaire with several hundred questions (can't remember which). The faculty had also taken this test and of all the students and staff who had taken it I had achieved the highest ever score (Strange but true!). So their expectation of me was as a clever guy and even when I was clearly wrong they still thought that there could be something of substance in what I was saying.

So find out how credible you are in a specific area in a specific context. We, for instance, are highly credible in the field of human behaviour in organisations; we have no credibility in sport and music for example. This prevents us from trying to influence in these fields but interestingly it doesn't stop some sport people and artists trying to influence outside of their chosen area, with very mixed results!

DEMONSTRATE INTEGRITY

To a large extent your ability to influence and convince others is also going to depend on how others view you from an ethical point of view, that is to what extent do they trust you? Clearly you are much more likely to be effective if you have developed a trusting relationship with those you seek to influence. Quite simply, if someone doesn't trust you, you are unlikely to be able to influence them. You may be able to order them to do something and you may be able to obtain compliance but you will not get commitment.

If I'm searching to buy a used book on Amazon or anything on Ebay, the thing which influences me most (apart from the price and product mix) is to what extent I trust the seller. The only way to know is to look at the reviews, and although good peer reviews are no guarantee, I can assure you I will not buy from someone with poor reviews.

So, how do I get people to trust me?

Trust has to be earned – you can't force someone to trust you – so you have to keep your word and be seen to keep your word. Organisations are like EBay in many respects; you only have to let one person down once and your reputation for not being trustworthy will grow (even if its not deserved). If I know you will keep your word (because you've kept it to me before or to others) then I will assume you will keep it again.

So how much does your target audience trust you? Maybe you need to spend time working on the relationships and developing trust before you start to try and influence a particular person or constituency?

DEVELOP RELATIONSHIPS

Psychologist Oliver James argues in his book, *They F*** You Up* that love creates crucial emotions far more effectively than fear.

In the case of Influencing it is our contention that effective relationships create an environment for successful influencing. So if I want to influence my boss, our relationship will be an important part of the mix. If it is positive and friendly then my boss is more likely to listen to what I say, I will be more confident in speaking up in the first place and probably be more assured in presenting my case. If however our relationship is poor and characterised by mutual dislike and mistrust then it is unlikely that I will be able to influence him or her very much. He/she will probably not listen to me, and even if he does he will probably dismiss what I say or mistrust my motives.

EXAMPLES

When I worked for a major US consulting company, I had a poor relationship with my boss and didn't respect or even listen to him. He had virtually no influence over me at all, apart form his obvious hierarchical power (which as we have already seen is often very limited).

Or take the case of John, a manager in an international company, whose employees complained to us that he was too busy to listen to them, and was abrupt and impersonal with them. They had little influence on him, and although he thought he had quite a strong influence on them, they did not respect him and therefore would not take his opinions seriously. Interestingly, when we interviewed them, they (the employees) blamed the manager, and the manager blamed his employees. In his opinion they were not as motivated or as serious as he was. It would have been more productive for all of them to have explored the quality of the relationship between them, than to have blamed each other.

So what can you do? The first thing is to take stock of your relationships – (look back at your Relationship Map. See Chapter 5, Awareness of Others)

How good are your relationships in general?

One of my colleagues asked me to do him a favour the other day which I was unable to do because of other commitments. I asked him if anyone else could step in and asked who his buddies were? His reply was interesting; he said that he didn't have that many. He had focussed on his work, his clients, and his research more than on creating internal networks. So he probably needs to work on his networks and relationships, because his ability to influence depends as much on that as it does on his own skills.

Look specifically at your relationships with your boss, key colleagues, peers, direct reports? How would you characterise them, on a scale of 1 to 10 with 10 being perfect and 1 awful? If you are not scoring more than 5 on most of them then you are in trouble when it comes to effective influence.

How about your clients, your family or your friends?

You need to think deeply about the quality of your relationships because this is the bedrock of effective influencing in the organisation. If they are not positive start working on them right away. Forget who is right and who is wrong and if you have had arguments. Get to know people better, ask them about their jobs, find out how you can help and support them. We both know people who have been technically brilliant and hardworking but who have lost their jobs through their inability to create positive relationships. In a networked organisation it is even more vital. You can succeed if you have poor relationships at work but are successful in what you are doing, but as soon as that performance slips you have no supporters or relationships and your days are numbered! Of course effective relationships will not protect you for ever from poor performance, but it will give you breathing space, or you will be helped and supported to perform more effectively or moved to a position where you can succeed.

So the lesson is, don't even start to influence someone if you have a poor or negative relationship. Start by working on the relationship and at least move it to neutral before trying to positively influence.

The Eight Influencing Misconceptions

There are a number of myths and misconceptions about Influencing all of which can derail you in your influencing processes. These are:

> **The hard sell is most effective**
> **Influencing is a one way process**
> **You must always succeed**
> **Compromise is weakness**
> **The best argument wins**
> **Being right is enough**
> **'It's their fault'**
> **Influencing is about manipulating people**

THE HARD SELL IS MOST EFFECTIVE

As I've been writing this at home today I have had two phone calls both from organisations trying to influence me to buy something. One was successful and one was not. Among other things the one that was not successful tried a hard sell, manipulative approach. I had to answer the question, 'if I wanted to replace any doors in my house at no cost at all, how many would I replace?' Now I've already been caught out by this question (it's a very popular approach by double glazing companies) and had answered truthfully in the past. Unfortunately the bit about being no cost is misleading nonsense, and once you've admitted that you have doors/windows/kitchens to replace you're halfway to being sold the product! I also did not like the sales person's voice (not clear) and speed of delivery (too fast).

The correct answer in these cases is always, 'None, I've just had them all replaced'. The second company was more successful; no trick questions but a straightforward one about how often I read a particular quality daily newspaper. The voice was articulate and friendly and relaxed and I felt no hard sell. This is a newspaper I read at least once a week including Sundays and the offer was clear and interesting. So I agreed to their offer of a cheaper subscription. However if I had felt a hard sell I would have hung up the phone. Clearly there were two major things in play here. One was the fact that I already knew and read the newspaper. So they had high credibility as far as I was concerned, plus I trusted them (for some reason I am unwilling to trust most of the double glazing, kitchen and telephone companies that call me!).

INFLUENCING IS A ONE WAY PROCESS

Effective influencing is not a one way process; it is an ongoing and multi directional process. This is very important to remember. There are exceptions to this, door to door selling for example and situations where you will never see the other person again. However for most of us influencing takes place in the context of ongoing relationships. We will see the other people again and it is important for the influencer to be open to being influenced by others. You will not always be right and you need to have a reputation as an open flexible person, someone who although an effective influencer is open to others' points of view. Counter intuitively this will make you a more effective influencer.

YOU MUST ALWAYS SUCCEED

You won't, quite simply, but that shouldn't put you off trying. Sometimes you win, sometimes you lose. The goal is not to fully influence everyone all of the time but to become a more effective Influencer. Often you have to choose your influence battles, because sometimes the odds are not on your side or it is politically expedient not to win.

A personal example is that recently I was travelling home from a seminar I was running in Paris. I was at Charles de Gaulle airport at three in the afternoon, waiting for a plane at four twenty. Coincidently there was an important Rugby match I wanted to see – Scotland versus France. There were no television screens in the departure lounge and the only possibility of seeing this match seemed to be in the business lounge of the airline with which I was travelling. I was not travelling business class, didn't have a gold card (But I did have a Frequent Flyer membership) and I didn't think I would have much chance of getting in. Still if you don't try you don't get! Or in this case, you don't influence!

My hope was that the lounge would be pretty much empty, the host or hostess sympathetic, and my approach would be very low key and hopeful. I went to the lounge, which was empty, admitted that in this case I was not flying business, and that I knew I had no right to come into the lounge, but explained that my national team was playing rugby, and there were no other televisions, and since the lounge was empty perhaps he wouldn't mind if I came in and watched TV for a little while and that I wouldn't eat or drink anything.

The guy looked at me in what I can only describe as smug superior sort of way and said that only customers with business class tickets could use the business class lounge! I smiled and said I realised this, and was just kind of hoping that he could make a one off exception today, especially since the place was deserted. But I could see that this was not going to work; he had his rules and exceptions were clearly not part of his vocabulary. He didn't smile, say sorry he'd like to help but couldn't, just continued to look smug. I could have come up with more arguments, pleaded etc. but it was never going to work. I intuitively knew that if I continued we would get into an argument and that he was likely to even call in security. So I remained polite, thanked him anyway and left.

I consider myself a good influencer and I always *try* to influence, and maybe you can come up with other arguments that would have been effective. But the key lesson is, you don't always succeed and you need to know when to stop. Otherwise you lose credibility, or you irritate people.

Now I won't hold this against the airline; I fully understand that they can't on principle allow non business class passengers into the business class lounge and I wouldn't even have tried probably if it had been busy. But I do hold it against their employee on that afternoon because he did not have the graciousness even to be understanding and friendly in his refusal, just the smugness and pettiness of someone wielding a little bit of power. Another afternoon and a different person and I may have been lucky, but at least I got to try my skills (or lack of them in this example). And practice makes more perfect than not practising!

COMPROMISE IS WEAKNESS

This is absolute nonsense; compromise is absolutely necessary for successful influencing. Quite simply to refuse to compromise is to admit you do not wish to influence but to get people to do what you want them to do and in your way. Influencing is all about working together to manoeuvre through a process, giving and taking along the way. While writing this book we have had to compromise frequently; we are both pretty strong characters, with our own thoughts, ideas and opinions both about influencing and about book writing. When we compromise it is usually following a robust discussion about the issue where aspects of both our ideas and approaches have been incorporated in what or how we are writing. In the end compromise feels good as it means all parties (or in our case both parties) can feel equally satisfied that their views have been taken into consideration.

Another aspect to compromising is that, although it may not lead to the best possible result, it has its place in the overall process of influencing. Of course there are some issues on which you may not wish to compromise, but people who never ever compromise are seen as rigid, inflexible and unrealistic.

THE BEST ARGUMENT WINS

Many of the managers and executives we meet are very logical people; they pride themselves on their ability to influence by putting together a rational, objective and well thought through argument. They are often experts in their own area and truly believe that having done their homework the case they put forward to others will be seen as the obvious way ahead. Where they most often fall down is that they forget to consider the other person's perspective and point of view and rarely if ever do they consider the emotional aspect of influencing. Let us say it again, 'logic is not enough'.

BEING RIGHT IS ENOUGH

We meet so many managers who tell us that their issue in influencing is that they are right but the others don't understand. One manager even told us 'I need to understand how to get people to accept that I am right. Currently they don't but when it comes down to it I nearly always am!' Well, sorry but we have to tell you here and now 'being right is not enough'. Yes, its not fair and in an ideal world it would be good enough. The fact is you can be as right as you like but unless you convince the others you are right you are wrong. And even if you are wrong and can convince others then you are right!

'I told you so' is a common but useless phrase. If you have ever said that then kick yourself because you have missed a good opportunity to influence others!

In our different sessions and team exercises at Ashridge we often see people who have the correct solution to a problem. But they are not capable of communicating this effectively to the other members of the group. It may be that they lack confidence, or are rather introverted, or unsure of themselves. Maybe English is not their first language and they are unsure of what to say. The team might be dominated by extraverts, or people who are not good listeners (this happens often!) So they have the answer but are unable to influence the others. Clearly the others in the group are at fault in the sense that they should learn to listen better and to probe more effectively. But at the end of the day, it is your responsibility to learn how to communicate and influence in an effective manner. When the exercise is finished and we debrief the groups, one person will often say, 'Yes I thought that was the right answer'. To which we will reply, 'Then what prevented you from attempting to influence the group?'

So the lesson is, if you are shy and introverted then work on your communication, and if you are extroverted and confident then work on your listening and probing skills!

'ITS THEIR FAULT'

Many participants and managers we have observed believe that if they do not manage to effectively influence another person or group then it's that person's fault. 'They don't understand', or 'they are stupid' are typical reactions. Well it actually doesn't matter if they are stupid, you cannot do anything about that! What you can do something about is changing your approach. You will always learn something from a person's or group's refusal to be influenced. This will give you a clue as to how to change your approach.

Responsibility is the key word here. Don't project onto others; take responsibility for your actions. If you are not getting through, then be flexible and change your approach. Be honest with yourself. How flexible are you really? How much preparation have you done? Take a long hard look at your influencing styles and strategies. You can change these. What you cannot do is change the other person!

INFLUENCING IS ABOUT MANIPULATING PEOPLE

Again many of our participants feel that if they try to influence others they are somehow being unethical and manipulating others. Clearly there are times when you could influence in an unethical way; if you tell lies for example, or are deliberately seeking to harm someone. But most times influencing is a natural part of communication.

As we have pointed out in the Introduction, we influence others every single day of our lives and in fact we have always influenced others from our earliest childhood onwards. In fact *not* influencing others could be regarded as unethical; if you believe something is right is it not your duty to influence them? If you saw something wrong you would try to influence the person doing something wrong, wouldn't you?

As long as you are not trying to manipulate other people, as long as you are not abusing power, as long as you are being truthful, it is perfectly ethical to try to influence others.

Ten Top Tips

Our final message relates to what we believe to be the ten top tips for effective influencing.

> **Be patient**
> **Active listening**
> **Flexibility**
> **Build and link**
> **Show understanding for others**
> **Express yourself fluently**
> **Check understanding**
> **Be energetic and enthusiastic**
> **Remember the unextinguished fire**
> **Above all plan and prepare**

Be patient

This is possibly the most important aspect of successful influencing. Influencing is not a one off event but a process which happens over a period of time and therefore demands a degree of patience by the influencer. Influencing is essentially about developing relationships. Relationship development demands both skill and patience to get things right. Every time you have an interaction with someone who is in your influencing network, whether you are attempting to influence them or not, you are having an impact on them and leaving them with an impression of you. Bearing this in mind and recognising that every interaction you take part in will have an affect upon your overall relationship with an individual should serve you well in developing long-term and beneficial influencing relationships.

Active listening

It is often cited as one of the key skills for success in many different interpersonal processes. As far as influencing is concerned, to actively listen involves a process of questioning, observing and listening to establish understanding. Truly effective listening behaviour is demanding and tiring. Focussing on what another person is saying and giving them your undivided attention is difficult. There are so many distractions, other conversations, telephones ringing, Emails to answer, your to do list, your own thought processes to name but a few. Practising and developing your skill in this area, getting feedback from others on how you come across as a listener and becoming regarded by others as a good listener will give you real advantage in influencing discussions. Others are far more likely to listen to you if you listen to them!

Flexibility

Influencing involves adaptability where all parties have to be aware of the need to adapt to each others' ideas. As we have shown influencing is not about getting your own way. Rather it is about sharing, adapting and adjusting so that all parties involved feel that they have contributed to the outcome and to some extent have met their needs and 'got their way'. This means that we have to be flexible to be able to deal with others' needs and ways of operating, to adjust our own processes, approaches and style to match and work with others in an effective way. When influencing the most important issue is to reach an acceptable outcome for all involved, and to gain commitment to that outcome. This will most certainly mean that you cannot work without being flexible to the needs and demands of others.

Building and linking

In order to ensure flexibility and adaptability it is important to build on each others' ideas and to link and develop ideas together. This neat little technique helps to demonstrate both active listening and flexibility. By listening to others' comments and recognising what they are saying as something you can build on you will be both complimenting them on their idea but also building on it to incorporate some of your own ideas. In using this technique it is important to label its use by saying something like 'I like that idea and I'd like to build on it by adding ...' or simply 'I'd like to build on that ...'.

Show understanding for others

This involves establishing common ground by developing relations with others. Exploring ideas, listening and building open relationships will demonstrate understanding for others. The important aspect of this one is the actual demonstration of your understanding of the others' perspective. You may be understanding them in your head but not actually showing them that you have understood. So many of us listen, think that we understand and then quickly move on to add our own thoughts. Taking a few extra minutes to actually demonstrate that you have listened and understood by, for instance, asking some probing questions to develop the topic further or summarising in your own words will both demonstrate that you are getting it from the other person's perspective as well as your own. Using comments on feelings can also be useful here. For instance, saying something like 'I can see this is something you feel strongly about' or 'Your commitment to this issue is clear to see'. The important issue is the flagging and demonstration that you do actually understand them and their perspective.

Express yourself fluently

This is about how you express yourself using the variety of media at your disposal. It is important for successful influencers to develop the ability to express themselves both in factual and emotional terms. As we have shown expression comes from more than simply words but also from the way you say things and from your body language while involved in interactions. How you express yourself in terms of the various media you use when communicating also has an impact on the message you are trying to convey. Fluent expression is about the way you convey the whole message, not simply how you use words, paralanguage and body language, but also the methods you use. The approach, a formal or informal presentation, an Email, a telephone conversation, etc. and the supporting material you use for instance, power point slides, photographs, examples of the real thing, videos, compact disks, etc. will have a significant impact on how you express yourself and upon how you are perceived by others in delivering your message.

Test understanding

As well as demonstrating understanding of others it is vital to check that others are moving with you and working in empathy with you. Testing understanding involves listening to the other party's perspectives followed by a replay of their message using summary and clarification to ensure your understanding. However, to test true understanding one really ought to assess the level of empathy that exists between yourself and the others throughout the discussions. This is the important aspect that is often forgotten; you must test understanding throughout the whole process to ensure that you are moving forward together.

Be energetic and enthusiastic

Demonstrating enthusiasm and energy for your ideas indicates your belief. However, enthusiasm must be genuine, not fake. Others will quickly pick up on false belief and enthusiasm. Authentic energy and enthusiasm are demonstrated through a whole variety of means but mainly through the actual delivery of your message. After all, if you can't be enthusiastic about your ideas, who will be? This seems rather obvious doesn't it? But we can assure you that we see hundreds of managers who claim to be enthusiastic about an idea, a product or a service, but who fail dismally to convey that enthusiasm!

Beware the unextinguished fire

By this we mean it is important to understand that it only takes one dissenting person to cast doubts, as influencing is a highly complex and challenging process, more often than not involving multiple stakeholders. Failing to consider all the stakeholders during the process can lead to dissenters appearing at any stage. Obviously it is pretty difficult to ensure no dissenters; however, as with so many other aspects of the process, awareness is the key.

There is another aspect to the unextinguished fire; often in influencing situations you are so keen to get agreement that you fail to fully take into account the objections that others might have. So you push your argument forward, brushing aside, or just not listening to objections. So the others are not fully convinced, but rather than voice their disagreement they will shrug their shoulders and let it pass. This is not full agreement, leave alone total commitment. But the others in the team may not have the energy to fully voice their lack of agreement at that moment. Perhaps they don't really agree with you but they do not see the full implications of your decision at that moment. However when the decision comes to implementation, and your colleagues see how it will affect them, then the lack of full involvement, the failure to hear all their objections comes into play. This is where they start to disagree with you and voice their objections much more strongly. You are surprised, and tell them so. You thought that they had agreed with you. Why didn't they say all this at the meeting? 'We did', they reply, 'but you didn't listen! You didn't want to hear our objections'. This is the unextinguished fire. Like a fire, if it is not completely extinguished, it will flare up again. So too do objections if they are not fully explored.

Preparation and planning

Above everything else preparation and planning are key to success. Time spent in planning and preparation can of course help with all aspects of the process. Planning your overall approach is a good starting position; however many of us start well and forget to continue. If influencing is a process not an event then planning and preparation must take place throughout the process and not simply at the outset.

EXERCISE

Reflect about each of the ten tips and about your own personal skill as an influencer on each of them.

Top tips	Low Skill High Skill 1 2 3 4 5 6 7 8 9 10
How patient are you?	1 2 3 4 5 6 7 8 9 10
How good a listener are you?	1 2 3 4 5 6 7 8 9 10
How flexible are you?	1 2 3 4 5 6 7 8 9 10
To what extent do you build and link on others' ideas?	1 2 3 4 5 6 7 8 9 10
How empathetic are you in reality?	1 2 3 4 5 6 7 8 9 10
How expressive are you?	1 2 3 4 5 6 7 8 9 10
How effective are you at testing understanding?	1 2 3 4 5 6 7 8 9 10
How much energy and enthusiasm do you display?	1 2 3 4 5 6 7 8 9 10
How open are you to be challenged?	1 2 3 4 5 6 7 8 9 10
How effective are you at planning and preparation?	1 2 3 4 5 6 7 8 9 10

Now examine your scores and make notes about how you can develop your skill in any of the ten areas where you believe you need to grow.

....
....
....
....
....
....
....
....
....
....
....
....
....
....
....
....
....
....
....

These ten principles do not guarantee you success; however, taken together with other tips and techniques from this book they should contribute to greater effectiveness when influencing others. Finally you should remember really great influencers are also open to being influenced themselves –

it's a two way process!

Bibliography

Ansari, M. A. (1990) *Managing People at Work. Leadership Styles and Influencing Strategies.* Sage.

Arden, P. (2003) *Its not How Good You Are, It's How Good You Want To Be.* Phaidon Press.

Atkinson, M. (1986) *Our Masters' Voices.* Methuen.

Bandler, R. and La Valle, J. (1996) *Persuasion Engineering.* Meta Publications.

Beck, D. and Cowan, C. (1996) *Spiral Dynamics–Mastering Values, Leadership and Change.* Blackwell.

Birdwhistle, R. and Alfred R. Lindesmith (1999). *Social Psychology.* Sage.

Block, P. (1987) *The Empowered Manager.* Jossey Bass.

Bloom, H. (1994) *The Western Canon.* Papermac. Macmillan.

Boden, A. (1997) *The Cultural Gaffes Pocketbook.* Management Pocketbooks.

Bragg, M. (2004) *The Adventure of English.* Hodder & Stroughton.

Bragg, M.(1996) *Reinventing Influence.* Pitman Publishing.

Brent, M. (2005) To Use or Not To Use Shakespeare In Management Development? *Ashridge Training Journal,* October, 2005.

Bryson, B. (2003) *A Short History of Nearly Everything.* Black Swan.

Burns, R. (1994) *The Collected Poems of Robert Burns.* Wordsworth Editions.

Cialdini, R. B. (1993) *Influence. The Psychology of Persuasion.* Quill.

Conger, J. (1998) *Winning 'Em Over. A New Model for Management in the Age of Persuasion.* Simon and Schuster.

Covey, S. (2004) *The Seven Habits of Highly Effective People; Powerful lessons in Personal Change.* Free Press.

Crainer, S. (1997) *The Ultimate Book of Business Quotations.* Capstone Publishing Ltd.

Cram, T. O. (2001) *The Power of Relationship Marketing.* Financial Times and Prentice Hall.

Dawkins, P. (1998) *The Wisdom of Shakespeare in the Merchant of Venice.* IC Media Productions.

Dent, F. (2000) *Influence and Succeed.* David Grant Publishing.

Dent, F. and Brent, M. (2001) Influencing: A New Model. *Training Journal,* July.

Eales-White, R. (1997) *The Power of Persuasion*. Kogan Page.

Etzioni, A. (1993) *The Spirit of Community*. Crown.

Goleman, D. (1999) *Working with Emotional Intelligence*. Bloomsbury Paperbacks.

Grint, K. (1997) *Fuzzy Management*. OUP.

Harrison, R. (1972) Understanding Your Organisation's Character. *Harvard Business Review*, May–June.

Handy, C. (1985) *Understanding Organisations*. Penguin.

Hargie, O. and Dickson, D. (2004) *Skilled Interpersonal Communication*. Routledge.

Herrmann, N. (1993) *The Creative Brain*. Brain Books.

Hofstede, G. (1994) *Cultures and Organisations*. Harper Collins Business.

Hofstede, G. (2002) *Culture's Consequences*. Sage.

Hogan, K. (1998) *The Psychology of Persuasion. How to Persuade Others to Your Way of Thinking*. Pelican.

Huczynski, A. (1996) *Influencing within Organisations*. Prentice Hall.

IC Media productions.

James, O. (2003) *They F*** You Up. How to Survive Family Life*. Bloomsbury Publishing.

Jenkins, R. (2001) *Churchill*. Macmillan.

Jensen, R. (1999) *The Dream Society*. McGraw Hill.

Kanter, R. M. (1989) *When Giants Learn To Dance*. Allen and Unwin.

Kipnis, D., Schmidt, Stuart M., Swaffin-Smith, C., and Wilkinson, I. (1984) Patterns of Managerial Influence: Shotgun Managers, Tacticians, and Bystanders. *Organisational Dynamics*, 12(3): 58–67.

Kipnis, D., Schmidt, Stuart M., and Wilkinson, I. (1980) Intra Organisational Influence Tactics: Explorations in Getting One's Way. *Journal of Applied Psychology*, 65.

Levesque, P. (1995) *The WOW Factory*. Irwin Professional Publishing.

Lukes, S. (2005) *Power – A Radical View*. Palgrave.

MacArthur, B. (ed.) (1999) *The Penguin Book of 20th Century Speeches*. Penguin.

Magruder Watkins, J. and Mohr, B. J. (2001) *Appreciative Inquiry*. Jossey Bass/Pfeiffer.

Martin, J. (1997) Robert Reich's Labor Pains, *Fortune* (12 May).

Mattock, J. (1999) *The Cross Cultural Business Pocketbook*. Management Pocketbooks.

Mehrabian, A. (1977) *Non Verbal Communication*. W de Guyter.

Mills, H. (2000) *Artful Persuasion*. Amacom.

Mortensen, K. W. (2004) *Maximum Influence: The 12 Universal Laws of Power Persuasion*. Amacom.

O' Connor, J. (2001) *NLP Workbook*. Element.

Olivier, R. (2001) *Inspirational Leadership*. The Industrial Society.

Pfeffer, J. (1992) *Managing with Power; Politics and Influence in Organisations*. Harvard Business School Press.

Pine, B. and Gilmore, J. (1999) *The Experience Economy*. Harvard Business Press.

Prince, G. M. (1970) *The Practise of Creativity*. Collier Books.

Sanders, R. and Fitch, K. (2001) The Actual Practise of Compliance seeking. *Communication Theory* 11 (3).

Semler, R. (2001) *Maverick*. Random House Business Books.

Shakespeare, W. (1996) *Henry V*, Penguin.

Trompenaars, F. and Hampden-Turner, C. (1997) *Riding The Waves Of Culture: Understanding Cultural Diversity In Business*. Nicholas Brealey Publishing.

Twain, M. (1994) *The Adventures of Tom Sawyer*. Penguin Popular Classics.

Watkins, J. and Mohr, B. (2001) *Appreciative Inqury: Change at the Speed of Imagination*. Jossey Bass/Pfeiffer.

Watzlawick, P. *et al.* (1980) *Change: Principles of Problem Formation and Problem Resolution*. WW Norton & Co.

Wilber, K. (2000) *Integral Pyschology*. Shambhala Publications.

Yukl, G. (1989) *Leadership in Organisation*. Prentice Hall.

Other resources

QUESTIONNAIRES

▶ Ashridge Inventory Of Management Skills – AIMS – The Emotional Element
▶ The Influencing Style Questionnaire
  Both available from:
    Ashridge
    Ashridge Psychometric Services
    Berkhamsted
    Herts
    HP4 1NS
  www.ashridge.org.uk
▶ For Hermann Split Brain Dominance Instrument contact Sally Bishop on 0044 1424 775 100
  www.hdbi.co.uk

Index